Helen Ingham
Naw Ruz 149

Tablets
of
Bahá'u'lláh

revealed after the Kitáb-i-Aqdas

D1125685

Tablets
of
Bahá'u'lláh

revealed after the Kitáb-i-Aqdas

*Compiled by the Research Department of
the Universal House of Justice
and translated by
Habib Taherzadeh
with the assistance of a Committee
at the Bahá'í World Centre*

BAHÁ'Í PUBLISHING TRUST
WILMETTE, ILLINOIS 60091

Bahá'í Publishing Trust, Wilmette, IL 60091

Library of Congress Cataloging-in-Publication Data

Bahá' Alláh, 1817–1892.
   Tablets of Bahá'u'lláh, revealed after the Kitáb-i-aqdas.

   Bibliography: p.
   Includes index.
   1. Bahai Faith—Doctrines. I. Taherzadeh, Habib.
II. Universal House of Justice. Research Dept.
III. Title.
BP360.B11913   1988   297'.8982   88-6250
ISBN 0-87743-216-3

Tablets of Bahá'u'lláh was first issued in 1978 in a hardcover edition (ISBN 0-85398-077-2) by the Bahá'í World Centre, Haifa, Israel. A lightweight edition (ISBN 0-85398-137-X), with many corrections and an index, was issued in 1982. The first pocket-sized edition was released in 1988 by permission of the Bahá'í World Centre.

Cover design by John Solarz

PREFACE

'The formulation by Bahá'u'lláh, in His *Kitáb-i-Aqdas*, of the fundamental laws of His Dispensation was followed, as His Mission drew to a close, by the enunciation of certain precepts and principles which lie at the very core of His Faith, by the reaffirmation of truths He had previously proclaimed, by the elaboration and elucidation of some of the laws He had already laid down, by the revelation of further prophecies and warnings, and by the establishment of subsidiary ordinances designed to supplement the provisions of His Most Holy Book. These were recorded in unnumbered Tablets, which He continued to reveal until the last days of His earthly life, ... These Tablets—mighty and final effusions of His indefatigable pen—must rank among the choicest fruits which His mind has yielded, and mark the consummation of His forty-year-long ministry.'[1]

Six of the Tablets referred to in the above passage and which are included in this volume, were, on the instructions of 'Abdu'l-Bahá, translated into English and published, in 1917, by Bahá'í Publishing Society, Chicago. That volume has long been out of print and its contents are now known to most Bahá'ís only through excerpts printed in compilations or quoted in other writings. Moreover, as Shoghi Effendi's translations of the Sacred Text increasingly flowed from his pen, it became apparent that the earlier translations could well be improved, both in accuracy and style. The Universal House of Justice therefore commis-

[1] Shoghi Effendi, *God Passes By* (Bahá'í Publishing Trust, Wilmette, Ill. 1944, page 216).

sioned this volume, which it describes as yet one more attempt to render into adequate English Bahá'u'lláh's matchless utterance. Wherever any portion of the text had already been translated by the Guardian, that translation has been used. These passages are identified by the Notes at the end of the book.

References to the Qur'án

In footnotes referring to the Qur'án the súrihs have been numbered according to the original, whereas the verse numbers are those in Rodwell's translation which differ sometimes from those of the Arabic.

CONTENTS

1

LAWḤ-I-KARMIL
(Tablet of Carmel)

LL glory be to this Day, the Day in which the fragrances of mercy have been wafted over all created things, a Day so blest that past ages and centuries can never hope to rival it, a Day in which the countenance of the Ancient of Days hath turned towards His holy seat. Thereupon the voices of all created things, and beyond them those of the Concourse on High, were heard calling aloud: 'Haste thee, O Carmel, for lo, the light of the countenance of God, the Ruler of the Kingdom of Names and Fashioner of the heavens, hath been lifted upon thee.'

Seized with transports of joy, and raising high her voice, she thus exclaimed: 'May my life be a sacrifice to Thee, inasmuch as Thou hast fixed Thy gaze upon me, hast bestowed upon me Thy bounty, and hast directed towards me Thy steps. Separation from Thee, O Thou Source of everlasting life, hath well nigh consumed me, and my remoteness from Thy presence hath burned away my soul. All praise be to Thee for having enabled me to hearken to Thy call, for having honoured me with Thy footsteps, and for having quickened my soul through the vitalizing fragrance of Thy Day and the shrilling voice of Thy Pen, a voice Thou didst ordain as Thy trumpet-call amidst Thy people. And when the hour at which Thy resistless Faith was to be made manifest did strike, Thou didst breathe a breath of Thy spirit into Thy Pen, and lo, the entire creation shook to its very foundations, unveiling to mankind such mysteries as lay hidden within the treasuries of Him Who is the Possessor of all created things.'

No sooner had her voice reached that most exalted Spot than We made reply: 'Render thanks unto thy Lord, O Carmel. The fire of thy separation from Me was fast consuming thee, when the ocean of My presence surged before thy face, cheering thine eyes and those of all creation, and filling with delight all things visible and invisible. Rejoice, for God hath in this Day established upon thee His throne, hath made thee the dawning-place of His signs and the dayspring of the evidences of His Revelation. Well is it with him that circleth around thee, that proclaimeth the revelation of thy glory, and recounteth that which the bounty of the Lord thy God hath showered upon thee. Seize thou the Chalice of Immortality in the name of thy Lord, the All-Glorious, and give thanks unto Him, inasmuch as He, in token of His mercy unto thee, hath turned thy sorrow into gladness, and transmuted thy grief into blissful joy. He, verily, loveth the spot which hath been made the seat of His throne, which His footsteps have trodden, which hath been honoured by His presence, from which He raised His call, and upon which He shed His tears.

'Call out to Zion, O Carmel, and announce the joyful tidings: He that was hidden from mortal eyes is come! His all-conquering sovereignty is manifest; His all-encompassing splendour is revealed. Beware lest thou hesitate or halt. Hasten forth and circumambulate the City of God that hath descended from heaven, the celestial Kaaba round which have circled in adoration the favoured of God, the pure in heart, and the company of the most exalted angels. Oh, how I long to announce unto every spot on the surface of the earth, and to carry to each one of its cities, the glad-tidings of this Revelation—a Revelation to which the heart of Sinai hath been attracted, and in whose name the Burning Bush is calling: "Unto God, the Lord of Lords, belong the kingdoms of earth and heaven." Verily this is the Day in which both land and sea rejoice at this announcement, the Day for which have been laid up those things which God, through a bounty beyond the ken of mortal mind or heart, hath destined for revelation. Ere long will God sail His Ark upon thee, and will manifest the people of Bahá who have been mentioned in the Book of Names.'

Sanctified be the Lord of all mankind, at the mention of Whose name all the atoms of the earth have been made to vibrate, and the Tongue of Grandeur hath been moved to disclose that which had been wrapt in His knowledge and lay concealed within the treasury of His might. He, verily, through the potency of His name, the Mighty, the All-Powerful, the Most High, is the ruler of all that is in the heavens and all that is on earth.

2

LAWḤ-I-AQDAS

(The Most Holy Tablet)[1]

---

[1] Sometimes referred to as *Tablet to the Christians*.

This is the Most Holy Tablet sent down from the holy kingdom unto the one who hath set his face towards the Object of the adoration of the world, He Who hath come from the heaven of eternity, invested with transcendent glory

In the name of the Lord, the Lord of great glory.

THIS is an Epistle from Our presence unto him whom the veils of names have failed to keep back from God, the Creator of earth and heaven, that his eyes may be cheered in the days of his Lord, the Help in Peril, the Self-Subsisting.

Say, O followers of the Son![1] Have ye shut out yourselves from Me by reason of My Name? Wherefore ponder ye not in your hearts? Day and night ye have been calling upon your Lord, the Omnipotent, but when He came from the heaven of eternity in His great glory, ye turned aside from Him and remained sunk in heedlessness.

Consider those who rejected the Spirit[1] when He came unto them with manifest dominion. How numerous the Pharisees who had secluded themselves in synagogues in His name, lamenting over their separation from Him, and yet when the portals of reunion were flung open and the divine Luminary shone resplendent from the Dayspring of Beauty, they disbelieved in God, the Exalted, the Mighty. They failed to attain His presence, notwithstanding that

[1] Jesus.

His advent had been promised them in the Book of Isaiah as well as in the Books of the Prophets and the Messengers. No one from among them turned his face towards the Dayspring of divine bounty except such as were destitute of any power amongst men. And yet, today, every man endowed with power and invested with sovereignty prideth himself on His Name. Moreover, call thou to mind the one who sentenced Jesus to death. He was the most learned of his age in his own country, whilst he who was only a fisherman believed in Him. Take good heed and be of them that observe the warning.

Consider likewise, how numerous at this time are the monks who have secluded themselves in their churches, calling upon the Spirit, but when He appeared through the power of Truth, they failed to draw nigh unto Him and are numbered with those that have gone far astray. Happy are they that have abandoned them and set their faces towards Him Who is the Desire of all that are in the heavens and all that are on the earth.

They read the Evangel and yet refuse to acknowledge the All-Glorious Lord, notwithstanding that He hath come through the potency of His exalted, His mighty and gracious dominion. We, verily, have come for your sakes, and have borne the misfortunes of the world for your salvation. Flee ye the One Who hath sacrificed His life that ye may be quickened? Fear God, O followers of the Spirit, and walk not in the footsteps of every divine that hath gone far astray. Do ye imagine that He seeketh His own interests, when He hath, at all times, been threatened by the swords of the enemies; or that He seeketh the vanities of the world, after He hath been imprisoned in the most desolate of cities? Be fair in your judgement and follow not the footsteps of the unjust.

Open the doors of your hearts. He Who is the Spirit verily standeth before them. Wherefore banish ye Him Who hath purposed to draw you nigh unto a Resplendent Spot? Say: We, in truth, have opened unto you the gates of the Kingdom. Will ye bar the doors of your houses in My face? This indeed is naught but a grievous error. He, verily, hath again come down from heaven, even as He came down from it the first time. Beware lest ye dispute that which He proclaimeth, even as the people before you disputed His utterances. Thus instructeth you the True One, could ye but perceive it.

The river Jordan is joined to the Most Great Ocean, and the Son, in the holy vale, crieth out: 'Here am I, here am I O Lord, my God!', whilst Sinai circleth round the House, and the Burning Bush calleth aloud: 'He Who is the Desired One is come in His transcendent majesty.' Say, Lo! The Father is come, and that which ye were promised in the Kingdom is fulfilled! This is the Word which the Son concealed, when to those around Him He said: 'Ye cannot bear it now.' And when the appointed time was fulfilled and the Hour had struck, the Word shone forth above the horizon of the Will of God. Beware, O followers of the Son, that ye cast it not behind your backs. Take ye fast hold of it. Better is this for you than all that ye possess. Verily He is nigh unto them that do good. The Hour which We had concealed from the knowledge of the peoples of the earth and of the favoured angels hath come to pass. Say, verily, He hath testified of Me, and I do testify of Him. Indeed, He hath purposed no one other than Me. Unto this beareth witness every fair-minded and understanding soul.

Though beset with countless afflictions, We summon the people unto God, the Lord of names. Say, strive ye to

attain that which ye have been promised in the Books of
God, and walk not in the way of the ignorant. My body
hath endured imprisonment that ye may be released from
the bondage of self. Set your faces then towards His
countenance and follow not the footsteps of every hostile
oppressor. Verily, He hath consented to be sorely abased
that ye may attain unto glory, and yet, ye are disporting
yourselves in the vale of heedlessness. He, in truth, liveth in
the most desolate of abodes for your sakes, whilst ye dwell
in your palaces.

Say, did ye not hearken to the Voice of the Crier, calling
aloud in the wilderness of the Bayán, bearing unto you the
glad-tidings of the coming of your Lord, the All-Merciful?
Lo! He is come in the sheltering shadow of Testimony,
invested with conclusive proof and evidence, and those
who truly believe in Him regard His presence as the
embodiment of the Kingdom of God. Blessed is the man
who turneth towards Him, and woe betide such as deny or
doubt Him.

Announce thou unto the priests: Lo! He Who is the
Ruler is come. Step out from behind the veil in the name of
thy Lord, He Who layeth low the necks of all men.
Proclaim then unto all mankind the glad-tidings of this
mighty, this glorious Revelation. Verily, He Who is the
Spirit of Truth is come to guide you unto all truth. He
speaketh not as prompted by His own self, but as bidden by
Him Who is the All-Knowing, the All-Wise.

Say, this is the One Who hath glorified the Son and hath
exalted His Cause. Cast away, O peoples of the earth, that
which ye have and take fast hold of that which ye are
bidden by the All-Powerful, He Who is the Bearer of the
Trust of God. Purge ye your ears and set your hearts
towards Him that ye may hearken to the most wondrous

Call which hath been raised from Sinai, the habitation of your Lord, the Most Glorious. It will, in truth, draw you nigh unto the Spot wherein ye will perceive the splendour of the light of His countenance which shineth above this luminous Horizon.

O concourse of priests! Leave the bells, and come forth, then, from your churches. It behoveth you, in this day, to proclaim aloud the Most Great Name among the nations. Prefer ye to be silent, whilst every stone and every tree shouteth aloud: 'The Lord is come in His great glory!'? Well is it with the man who hasteneth unto Him. Verily, he is numbered among them whose names will be eternally recorded and who will be mentioned by the Concourse on High. Thus hath it been decreed by the Spirit in this wondrous Tablet. He that summoneth men in My name is, verily, of Me, and he will show forth that which is beyond the power of all that are on earth. Follow ye the Way of the Lord and walk not in the footsteps of them that are sunk in heedlessness. Well is it with the slumberer who is stirred by the Breeze of God and ariseth from amongst the dead, directing his steps towards the Way of the Lord. Verily, such a man is regarded, in the sight of God, the True One, as a jewel amongst men and is reckoned with the blissful.

Say: In the East the light of His Revelation hath broken; in the West have appeared the signs of His dominion. Ponder this in your hearts, O people, and be not of those who have turned a deaf ear to the admonitions of Him Who is the Almighty, the All-Praised. Let the Breeze of God awaken you. Verily, it hath wafted over the world. Well is it with him that hath discovered the fragrance thereof and been accounted among the well-assured.

O concourse of bishops! Ye are the stars of the heaven of My knowledge. My mercy desireth not that ye should fall upon the earth. My justice, however, declareth: 'This is that which the Son hath decreed.' And whatsoever hath proceeded out of His blameless, His truth-speaking, trustworthy mouth, can never be altered. The bells, verily, peal out My Name, and lament over Me, but My spirit rejoiceth with evident gladness. The body of the Loved One yearneth for the cross, and His head is eager for the spear, in the path of the All-Merciful. The ascendancy of the oppressor can in no wise deter Him from His purpose. We have summoned all created things to attain the presence of thy Lord, the King of all names. Blessed is the man that hath set his face towards God, the Lord of the Day of Reckoning.

O concourse of monks! If ye choose to follow Me, I will make you heirs of My Kingdom; and if ye transgress against Me, I will, in My long-suffering, endure it patiently, and I, verily, am the Ever-Forgiving, the All-Merciful.

O land of Syria! What hath become of thy righteousness? Thou art, in truth, ennobled by the footsteps of thy Lord. Hast thou perceived the fragrance of heavenly reunion, or art thou to be accounted of the heedless?

Bethlehem is astir with the Breeze of God. We hear her voice saying: 'O most generous Lord! Where is Thy great glory established? The sweet savours of Thy presence have quickened me, after I had melted in my separation from Thee. Praised be Thou in that Thou hast raised the veils, and come with power in evident glory.' We called unto her from behind the Tabernacle of Majesty and Grandeur: 'O Bethlehem! This Light hath risen in the orient, and travelled towards the occident, until it reached thee in the evening of its life. Tell Me then: Do the sons recognize the Father, and acknowledge Him, or do they deny Him, even as the people aforetime denied Him (Jesus)?' Whereupon she cried out saying: 'Thou art, in truth, the All-Knowing, the Best-Informed.' Verily, We behold all created things moved to bear witness unto Us. Some know Us and bear witness, while the majority bear witness, yet know Us not.

Mount Sinai is astir with the joy of beholding Our countenance. She hath lifted her enthralling voice in glorification of her Lord, saying: 'O Lord! I sense the fragrance of Thy garment. Methinks Thou art near, invested with the signs of God. Thou hast ennobled these regions with Thy footsteps. Great is the blessedness of Thy people, could they but know Thee and inhale Thy sweet savours; and woe betide them that are fast asleep.'

Happy art thou who hast turned thy face towards My countenance, inasmuch as thou hast rent the veils asunder, hast shattered the idols and recognized thine eternal Lord. The people of the Qur'án have risen up against Us without any clear proof or evidence, tormenting Us at every moment with a fresh torment. They idly imagine that tribulations can frustrate Our Purpose. Vain indeed is that which they have imagined. Verily, thy Lord is the One Who ordaineth whatsoever He pleaseth.

I never passed a tree but Mine heart addressed it saying: 'O would that thou wert cut down in My name, and My body crucified upon thee.' We revealed this passage in the Epistle to the Sháh that it might serve as a warning to the followers of religions. Verily, thy Lord is the All-Knowing, the All-Wise.

Let not the things they have perpetrated grieve thee. Truly they are even as dead, and not living. Leave them unto the dead, then turn thy face towards Him Who is the Life-Giver of the world. Beware lest the sayings of the heedless sadden thee. Be thou steadfast in the Cause, and teach the people with consummate wisdom. Thus enjoineth thee the Ruler of earth and heaven. He is in truth the Almighty, the Most Generous. Ere long will God exalt thy remembrance and will inscribe with the Pen of Glory that which thou didst utter for the sake of His love. He is in truth the Protector of the doers of good.

Give My remembrance to the one named Murád and say: 'Blessed art thou, O Murád, inasmuch as thou didst cast away the promptings of thine own desire and hast followed Him Who is the Desire of all mankind.'

Say: Blessed the slumberer who is awakened by My Breeze. Blessed the lifeless one who is quickened through My reviving breaths. Blessed the eye that is solaced by gazing at My beauty. Blessed the wayfarer who directeth his steps towards the Tabernacle of My glory and majesty. Blessed the distressed one who seeketh refuge beneath the shadow of My canopy. Blessed the sore athirst who hasteneth to the soft-flowing waters of My loving-kindness. Blessed the insatiate soul who casteth away his selfish desires for love of Me and taketh his place at the banquet table which I have sent down from the heaven of divine bounty for My chosen ones. Blessed the abased one who layeth fast hold on the cord of My glory; and the needy one who entereth beneath the shadow of the Tabernacle of My wealth. Blessed the ignorant one who seeketh the fountain of My knowledge; and the heedless one who cleaveth to the cord of My remembrance. Blessed the soul that hath been raised to life through My quickening breath and hath gained admittance into My heavenly Kingdom. Blessed the man whom the sweet savours of reunion with Me have stirred and caused to draw nigh unto the Dayspring of My Revelation. Blessed the ear that hath heard and the tongue that hath borne witness and the eye that hath seen and recognized the Lord Himself, in His great glory and majesty, invested with grandeur and dominion. Blessed are they that have attained His presence. Blessed the man who hath sought enlightenment from the Day-Star of My Word. Blessed he who hath attired his head with the diadem of My love. Blessed is he who hath heard of My grief and hath arisen to aid Me among My people. Blessed is he who hath laid down his life in My path and hath borne manifold hardships for the sake of My Name. Blessed the man who, assured of My Word, hath arisen from among the dead to celebrate My praise. Blessed is he that hath been enraptured by My wondrous melodies and hath rent the veils asunder through the potency of My might. Blessed is he who hath remained faithful to My Covenant, and whom the things of the world have not kept back from attaining My Court of holiness. Blessed is the man who hath detached himself from all else but Me, hath soared in the atmosphere of My love, hath gained admittance into My Kingdom, gazed upon My realms of glory, quaffed the living waters of My bounty, hath drunk his fill from the heavenly river of My loving providence, acquainted himself with My Cause, apprehended that which I concealed within the treasury of My Words, and hath shone forth from the horizon of divine knowledge engaged in My praise and glorification. Verily, he is of Me. Upon him rest My mercy, My loving-kindness, My bounty and My glory.

3

BISHÁRÁT
(Glad-Tidings)

This is the Call of the All-Glorious which is proclaimed from the Supreme Horizon in the Prison of 'Akká

He is the Expounder, the All-Knowing,
the All-Informed.

GOD, the True One, testifieth and the Revealers of His names and attributes bear witness that Our sole purpose in raising the Call and in proclaiming His sublime Word is that the ear of the entire creation may, through the living waters of divine utterance, be purged from lying tales and become attuned to the holy, the glorious and exalted Word which hath issued forth from the repository of the knowledge of the Maker of the Heavens and the Creator of Names. Happy are they that judge with fairness.

O people of the earth!

The first Glad-Tidings

which the Mother Book hath, in this Most Great Revelation, imparted unto all the peoples of the world is that the law of holy war hath been blotted out from the Book. Glorified be the All-Merciful, the Lord of grace abounding, through Whom the door of heavenly bounty hath been flung open in the face of all that are in heaven and on earth.

The second Glad-Tidings

It is permitted that the peoples and kindreds of the world associate with one another with joy and radiance. O people! Consort with the followers of all religions in a spirit of friendliness and fellowship. Thus hath the day-star of His sanction and authority shone forth above the horizon of the decree of God, the Lord of the worlds.

The third Glad-Tidings

concerneth the study of divers languages. This decree hath formerly streamed forth from the Pen of the Most High: It behoveth the sovereigns of the world—may God assist them—or the ministers of the earth to take counsel together and to adopt one of the existing languages or a new one to be taught to children in schools throughout the world, and likewise one script. Thus the whole earth will come to be regarded as one country. Well is it with him who hearkeneth unto His Call and observeth that whereunto he is bidden by God, the Lord of the Mighty Throne.

The fourth Glad-Tidings

Should any of the kings—may God aid them—arise to protect and help this oppressed people, all must vie with one another in loving and in serving him. This matter is incumbent upon everyone. Well is it with them that act accordingly.

The fifth Glad-Tidings

In every country where any of this people reside, they

must behave towards the government of that country with loyalty, honesty and truthfulness. This is that which hath been revealed at the behest of Him Who is the Ordainer, the Ancient of Days.

It is binding and incumbent upon the peoples of the world, one and all, to extend aid unto this momentous Cause which is come from the heaven of the Will of the ever-abiding God, that perchance the fire of animosity which blazeth in the hearts of some of the peoples of the earth may, through the living waters of divine wisdom and by virtue of heavenly counsels and exhortations, be quenched, and the light of unity and concord may shine forth and shed its radiance upon the world.

We cherish the hope that through the earnest endeavours of such as are the exponents of the power of God—exalted be His glory—the weapons of war throughout the world may be converted into instruments of reconstruction and that strife and conflict may be removed from the midst of men.

The sixth Glad-Tidings

is the establishment of the Lesser Peace, details of which have formerly been revealed from Our Most Exalted Pen. Great is the blessedness of him who upholdeth it and observeth whatsoever hath been ordained by God, the All-Knowing, the All-Wise.

The seventh Glad-Tidings

The choice of clothing and the cut of the beard and its dressing are left to the discretion of men. But beware, O people, lest ye make yourselves the playthings of the ignorant.

The eighth Glad-Tidings

The pious deeds of the monks and priests among the followers of the Spirit[1]—upon Him be the peace of God—are remembered in His presence. In this Day, however, let them give up the life of seclusion and direct their steps towards the open world and busy themselves with that which will profit themselves and others. We have granted them leave to enter into wedlock that they may bring forth one who will make mention of God, the Lord of the seen and the unseen, the Lord of the Exalted Throne.

The ninth Glad-Tidings

When the sinner findeth himself wholly detached and freed from all save God, he should beg forgiveness and pardon from Him. Confession of sins and transgressions before human beings is not permissible, as it hath never been nor will ever be conducive to divine forgiveness. Moreover such confession before people results in one's humiliation and abasement, and God—exalted be His glory—wisheth not the humiliation of His servants. Verily He is the Compassionate, the Merciful. The sinner should, between himself and God, implore mercy from the Ocean of mercy, beg forgiveness from the Heaven of generosity and say:

O God, my God! I implore Thee by the blood of Thy true lovers who were so enraptured by Thy sweet utterance that they hastened unto the Pinnacle of Glory, the site of the most glorious martyrdom, and I beseech Thee by the mysteries which lie enshrined in Thy knowledge and by

[1] Jesus.

the pearls that are treasured in the ocean of Thy bounty to grant forgiveness unto me and unto my father and my mother. Of those who show forth mercy, Thou art in truth the Most Merciful. No God is there but Thee, the Ever-Forgiving, the All-Bountiful.

O Lord! Thou seest this essence of sinfulness turning unto the ocean of Thy favour and this feeble one seeking the kingdom of Thy divine power and this poor creature inclining himself towards the day-star of Thy wealth. By Thy mercy and Thy grace, disappoint him not, O Lord, nor debar him from the revelations of Thy bounty in Thy days, nor cast him away from Thy door which Thou hast opened wide to all that dwell in Thy heaven and on Thine earth.

Alas! Alas! My sins have prevented me from approaching the Court of Thy holiness and my trespasses have caused me to stray far from the Tabernacle of Thy majesty. I have committed that which Thou didst forbid me to do and have put away what Thou didst order me to observe.

I pray Thee by Him Who is the sovereign Lord of Names to write down for me with the Pen of Thy bounty that which will enable me to draw nigh unto Thee and will purge me from my trespasses which have intervened between me and Thy forgiveness and Thy pardon.

Verily, Thou art the Potent, the Bountiful. No God is there but Thee, the Mighty, the Gracious.

The tenth Glad-Tidings

As a token of grace from God, the Revealer of this Most Great Announcement, We have removed from the Holy Scriptures and Tablets the law prescribing the destruction of books.

The eleventh Glad-Tidings

It is permissible to study sciences and arts, but such sciences as are useful and would redound to the progress and advancement of the people. Thus hath it been decreed by Him Who is the Ordainer, the All-Wise.

The twelfth Glad-Tidings

It is enjoined upon every one of you to engage in some form of occupation, such as crafts, trades and the like. We have graciously exalted your engagement in such work to the rank of worship unto God, the True One. Ponder ye in your hearts the grace and the blessings of God and render thanks unto Him at eventide and at dawn. Waste not your time in idleness and sloth. Occupy yourselves with that which profiteth yourselves and others. Thus hath it been decreed in this Tablet from whose horizon the day-star of wisdom and utterance shineth resplendent.

The most despised of men in the sight of God are those who sit idly and beg. Hold ye fast unto the cord of material means, placing your whole trust in God, the Provider of all means. When anyone occupieth himself in a craft or trade, such occupation itself is regarded in the estimation of God as an act of worship; and this is naught but a token of His infinite and all-pervasive bounty.

The thirteenth Glad-Tidings

The men of God's House of Justice have been charged with the affairs of the people. They, in truth, are the

Trustees of God among His servants and the daysprings of authority in His countries.

O people of God! That which traineth the world is Justice, for it is upheld by two pillars, reward and punishment. These two pillars are the sources of life to the world. Inasmuch as for each day there is a new problem and for every problem an expedient solution, such affairs should be referred to the Ministers of the House of Justice that they may act according to the needs and requirements of the time. They that, for the sake of God, arise to serve His Cause, are the recipients of divine inspiration from the unseen Kingdom. It is incumbent upon all to be obedient unto them. All matters of State should be referred to the House of Justice, but acts of worship must be observed according to that which God hath revealed in His Book.

O people of Bahá! Ye are the dawning-places of the love of God and the daysprings of His loving-kindness. Defile not your tongues with the cursing and reviling of any soul, and guard your eyes against that which is not seemly. Set forth that which ye possess. If it be favourably received, your end is attained; if not, to protest is vain. Leave that soul to himself and turn unto the Lord, the Protector, the Self-Subsisting. Be not the cause of grief, much less of discord and strife. The hope is cherished that ye may obtain true education in the shelter of the tree of His tender mercies and act in accordance with that which God desireth. Ye are all the leaves of one tree and the drops of one ocean.

The fourteenth Glad-Tidings

It is not necessary to undertake special journeys to visit the resting-places of the dead. If people of substance and affluence offer the cost of such journeys to the House of Justice, it will be pleasing and acceptable in the presence of God. Happy are they that observe His precepts.

The fifteenth Glad-Tidings

Although a republican form of government profiteth all the peoples of the world, yet the majesty of kingship is one of the signs of God. We do not wish that the countries of the world should remain deprived thereof. If the sagacious combine the two forms into one, great will be their reward in the presence of God.

In former religions such ordinances as holy war, destruction of books, the ban on association and companionship with other peoples or on reading certain books had been laid down and affirmed according to the exigencies of the time; however, in this mighty Revelation, in this momentous Announcement, the manifold bestowals and favours of God have overshadowed all men, and from the horizon of the Will of the Ever-Abiding Lord, His infallible decree hath prescribed that which We have set forth above.

We yield praise unto God—hallowed and glorified be He—for whatsoever He hath graciously revealed in this blessed, this glorious and incomparable Day. Indeed if everyone on earth were endowed with a myriad tongues and were to continually praise God and magnify His Name to the end that knoweth no end, their thanksgiving would not prove adequate for even one of the gracious favours We have mentioned in this Tablet. Unto this beareth witness every man of wisdom and discernment, of understanding and knowledge.

We earnestly beseech God—exalted be His glory—to aid the rulers and sovereigns, who are the exponents of power and the daysprings of glory, to enforce His laws and ordinances. He is in truth the Omnipotent, the All-Powerful, He Who is wont to answer the call of men.

4

ṬARÁZÁT
(Ornaments)

In My Name, which standeth supreme above all names

PRAISE and glory beseem the Lord of Names and the Creator of the heavens, He, the waves of Whose ocean of Revelation surge before the eyes of the peoples of the world. The Day-Star of His Cause shineth through every veil and His Word of affirmation standeth beyond the reach of negation. Neither the ascendancy of the oppressor nor the tyranny of the wicked hath been able to thwart His Purpose. How glorified is His sovereignty, how exalted His dominion!

Great God! Although His signs have encompassed the world and His proofs and testimonies are shining forth and manifest as the light, yet the ignorant appear heedless, nay rather, rebellious. Would that they had been content with opposition. But at all times they are plotting to cut down the sacred Lote-Tree. Since the dawn of this Revelation the embodiments of selfishness have, by resorting to cruelty and oppression, striven to extinguish the Light of divine manifestation. But God, having stayed their hands, revealed this Light through His sovereign authority and protected it through the power of His might until earth and heaven were illumined by its radiance and brightness. Praise be unto Him under all conditions.

Glory be unto Thee, O Lord of the world and Desire of the nations, O Thou Who hast become manifest in the Greatest Name whereby the pearls of wisdom and utterance have appeared from the shells of the great sea of Thy knowledge, and the heavens of divine revelation have been adorned with the light of the appearance of the Sun of Thy countenance.

I beg of Thee, by that Word through which Thy proof was perfected among Thy creatures and Thy testimony was fulfilled among Thy servants to strengthen Thy people in that whereby the face of the Cause will radiate in Thy dominion, the standards of Thy power will be planted among Thy servants, and the banners of Thy guidance will be raised throughout Thy dominions.

O my Lord! Thou beholdest them clinging to the rope of Thy grace and holding fast unto the hem of the mantle of Thy beneficence. Ordain for them that which may draw them nearer unto Thee, and withhold them from all else save Thee. I beg of Thee, O Thou King of existence and Protector of the seen and the unseen, to make whosoever ariseth to serve Thy Cause as a sea moving by Thy desire, as one ablaze with the fire of Thy Sacred Tree, shining from the horizon of the heaven of Thy will. Verily Thou art the mighty One Whom neither the power of all the world nor the strength of nations can weaken. There is no God but Thee, the One, the Incomparable, the Protector, the Self-Subsistent.

O thou who hast quaffed the wine of Mine utterance from the chalice of My knowledge! These sublime words were heard today from the rustling of the divine Lote-Tree which the Lord of Names hath, with the hand of celestial power, planted in the All-Highest Paradise:

The first Ṭaráz

and the first effulgence which hath dawned from the horizon of the Mother Book is that man should know his own self and recognize that which leadeth unto loftiness or lowliness, glory or abasement, wealth or poverty. Having attained the stage of fulfilment and reached his maturity, man standeth in need of wealth, and such wealth as he acquireth through crafts or professions is commendable and praiseworthy in the estimation of men of wisdom, and especially in the eyes of servants who dedicate themselves to the education of the world and to the edification of its peoples. They are, in truth, cup-bearers of the life-giving water of knowledge and guides unto the ideal way. They direct the peoples of the world to the straight path and acquaint them with that which is conducive to human upliftment and exaltation. The straight path is the one which guideth man to the dayspring of perception and to the dawning-place of true understanding and leadeth him to that which will redound to glory, honour and greatness.

We cherish the hope that through the loving-kindness of the All-Wise, the All-Knowing, obscuring dust may be dispelled and the power of perception enhanced, that the people may discover the purpose for which they have been called into being. In this Day whatsoever serveth to reduce blindness and to increase vision is worthy of consideration. This vision acteth as the agent and guide for true knowledge. Indeed in the estimation of men of wisdom keenness of understanding is due to keenness of vision. The people of Bahá must under all circumstances observe that which is meet and seemly and exhort the people accordingly.

The second Ṭaráz

is to consort with the followers of all religions in a spirit of friendliness and fellowship, to proclaim that which the

Speaker on Sinai hath set forth and to observe fairness in all matters.

They that are endued with sincerity and faithfulness should associate with all the peoples and kindreds of the earth with joy and radiance, inasmuch as consorting with people hath promoted and will continue to promote unity and concord, which in turn are conducive to the maintenance of order in the world and to the regeneration of nations. Blessed are such as hold fast to the cord of kindliness and tender mercy and are free from animosity and hatred.

This Wronged One exhorteth the peoples of the world to observe tolerance and righteousness, which are two lights amidst the darkness of the world and two educators for the edification of mankind. Happy are they who have attained thereto and woe betide the heedless.

The third Ṭaráz

concerneth good character. A good character is, verily, the best mantle for men from God. With it He adorneth the temples of His loved ones. By My life! The light of a good character surpasseth the light of the sun and the radiance thereof. Whoso attaineth unto it is accounted as a jewel among men. The glory and the upliftment of the world must needs depend upon it. A goodly character is a means whereby men are guided to the Straight Path and are led to the Great Announcement. Well is it with him who is adorned with the saintly attributes and character of the Concourse on High.

It beseemeth you to fix your gaze under all conditions upon justice and fairness. In the Hidden Words this exalted utterance hath been revealed from Our Most August Pen:

'O Son of Spirit! The best beloved of all things in My

sight is Justice; turn not away therefrom if thou desirest Me, and neglect it not that I may confide in thee. By its aid thou shalt see with thine own eyes and not through the eyes of others, and shalt know of thine own knowledge and not through the knowledge of thy neighbour. Ponder this in thy heart; how it behoveth thee to be. Verily justice is My gift to thee and the sign of My loving-kindness. Set it then before thine eyes.'

They that are just and fair-minded in their judgement occupy a sublime station and hold an exalted rank. The light of piety and uprightness shineth resplendent from these souls. We earnestly hope that the peoples and countries of the world may not be deprived of the splendours of these two luminaries.

The fourth Ṭaráz

concerneth trustworthiness. Verily it is the door of security for all that dwell on earth and a token of glory on the part of the All-Merciful. He who partaketh thereof hath indeed partaken of the treasures of wealth and prosperity. Trustworthiness is the greatest portal leading unto the tranquillity and security of the people. In truth the stability of every affair hath depended and doth depend upon it. All the domains of power, of grandeur and of wealth are illumined by its light.

Not long ago these sublime words were revealed from the Pen of the Most High:

'We will now mention unto thee Trustworthiness and the station thereof in the estimation of God, thy Lord, the Lord of the Mighty Throne. One day of days We repaired unto Our Green Island. Upon Our arrival, We beheld its streams flowing, and its trees luxuriant, and the sunlight playing in their midst. Turning Our face to the right, We beheld what the pen is powerless to describe; nor can it set forth that which the eye of the Lord of Mankind witnessed in that most sanctified, that most sublime, that blest, and most exalted Spot. Turning, then, to the left We gazed on one of the Beauties of the Most Sublime Paradise, standing on a pillar of light, and calling aloud saying: "O inmates of earth and heaven! Behold ye My beauty, and My radiance, and My revelation, and My effulgence. By God, the True One! I am Trustworthiness and the revelation thereof, and the beauty thereof. I will recompense whosoever will cleave unto Me, and recognize My rank and station, and hold fast unto My hem. I am the most great ornament of the people of Bahá, and the vesture of glory unto all who are in the kingdom of creation. I am the supreme instrument for the prosperity of the world, and the horizon of assurance unto all beings." Thus have We sent down for thee that which will draw men nigh unto the Lord of creation.'

O people of Bahá! Trustworthiness is in truth the best of vestures for your temples and the most glorious crown for your heads. Take ye fast hold of it at the behest of Him Who is the Ordainer, the All-Informed.

The fifth Ṭaráz

concerneth the protection and preservation of the stations of God's servants. One should not ignore the truth of any matter, rather should one give expression to that which is right and true. The people of Bahá should not deny any soul the reward due to him, should treat craftsmen with deference, and, unlike the people aforetime, should not defile their tongues with abuse.

In this Day the sun of craftsmanship shineth above the horizon of the occident and the river of arts is flowing out of the sea of that region. One must speak with fairness and appreciate such bounty. By the life of God! The word 'Equity' shineth bright and resplendent even as the sun. We pray God to graciously shed its radiance upon everyone. He is in truth powerful over all things, He Who is wont to answer the prayers of all men.

In these days truthfulness and sincerity are sorely afflicted in the clutches of falsehood, and justice is tormented by the scourge of injustice. The smoke of corruption hath enveloped the whole world in such wise that naught can be seen in any direction save regiments of soldiers and nothing is heard from any land but the clashing of swords. We beseech God, the True One, to strengthen the wielders of His power in that which will rehabilitate the world and bring tranquillity to the nations.

The sixth Ṭaráz

Knowledge is one of the wondrous gifts of God. It is incumbent upon everyone to acquire it. Such arts and material means as are now manifest have been achieved by virtue of His knowledge and wisdom which have been revealed in Epistles and Tablets through His Most Exalted Pen—a Pen out of whose treasury pearls of wisdom and utterance and the arts and crafts of the world are brought to light.

In this Day the secrets of the earth are laid bare before the eyes of men. The pages of swiftly-appearing newspapers are indeed the mirror of the world. They reflect the deeds and the pursuits of divers peoples and kindreds. They both reflect them and make them known. They are a mirror endowed with hearing, sight and speech. This is an amazing and potent phenomenon. However, it behoveth the writers thereof to be purged from the promptings of evil passions and desires and to be attired with the raiment of justice and equity. They should enquire into situations as much as possible and ascertain the facts, then set them down in writing.

Concerning this Wronged One, most of the things reported in the newspapers are devoid of truth. Fair speech and truthfulness, by reason of their lofty rank and position, are regarded as a sun shining above the horizon of knowledge. The waves rising from this Ocean are apparent before the eyes of the peoples of the world and the effusions of the Pen of wisdom and utterance are manifest everywhere.

It is reported in the press that this Servant hath fled from the land of Ṭá (Ṭihrán) and gone to 'Iráq. Gracious God! Not even for a single moment hath this Wronged One ever concealed Himself. Rather hath He at all times remained steadfast and conspicuous before the eyes of all men. Never have We retreated, nor shall We ever seek flight. In truth it is the foolish people who flee from Our presence. We left Our home country accompanied by two mounted escorts, representing the two honoured governments of Persia and Russia until We arrived in 'Iráq in the plenitude of glory and power. Praise be to God! The Cause whereof this Wronged One is the Bearer standeth as high as heaven and shineth resplendent as the sun. Concealment hath no access unto this station, nor is there any occasion for fear or silence.

The mysteries of Resurrection and the events of the Last Hour are openly manifest, but the people are sunk in heedlessness and have suffered themselves to be wrapt in veils. 'And when the seas shall boil ... And when the Scriptures shall be unrolled.'[1] By the righteousness of God! The Dawn hath truly brightened and the light hath shone forth and the night hath receded. Happy are they that comprehend. Happy are they that have attained thereunto.

Glorified be God! The Pen is perplexed what to write and the Tongue wondereth what to utter. Despite unprecedented hardships and after enduring years of imprisonment, captivity and woeful trials, We now perceive that veils thicker than the ones We have already torn asunder have intervened, obstructing the vision and causing the light of understanding to be obscured. Moreover We observe that the fresh calumnies which are now rife are far more malicious than those of former days.

O people of the Bayán! Fear ye the merciful Lord. Consider the people of former times. What were their deeds and what fruit did they gather? Every thing they uttered was but imposture and whatever they wrought hath proved worthless, except for those whom God hath graciously protected through His power.

I swear by the life of Him Who is the Desire of the world! Were a man to ponder in his heart he would, free of all attachment to the world, hasten unto the Most Great Light and would purge and purify himself from the dust of vain imaginings and the smoke of idle fancy. What could have prompted the people of the past to err and by whom were they misled? They still reject the truth and have turned towards their own selfish desires. This Wronged One calleth aloud for the sake of God. Whosoever wisheth, let him turn thereunto; whosoever wisheth, let him turn away. Verily God can well afford to dispense with all things, whether of the past or of the future.

[1] Qur'án 81: 6 & 10.

O people of the Bayán! It is men like unto Hádí Dawlat-Ábádí[1] who, with turban and staff,[2] have been the source of opposition and hindrance and have so grievously burdened the people with superstitions that even at the present time they still expect the appearance of a fictitious person from a fictitious place. Be ye warned, O men of understanding.

O Hádí! Give ear unto the Voice of this trustworthy Counsellor: direct thy steps from the left unto the right, that is turn away from idle fancy unto certitude. Lead not the people into error. The divine Luminary shineth, His Cause is manifest and His signs are all-embracing. Set thy face towards God, the Help in Peril, the Self-Subsisting. Renounce thy leadership for the sake of God and leave the people unto themselves. Thou art ignorant of the essential truth, thou art not acquainted therewith.

O Hádí! Be thou of one face in the path of God. When in company with the infidels, thou art an infidel and with the pious, thou art pious. Reflect thou upon such souls as offered up their lives and their substance in that land, that haply thou mayest be admonished and roused from slumber. Consider: who is to be preferred, he who preserveth his body, his life and his possessions or the one who surrendereth his all in the path of God? Judge thou fairly and be not of the unjust. Take fast hold of justice and adhere unto equity that perchance thou mayest not, for selfish motives, use religion as a snare, nor disregard the truth for the sake of gold. Indeed thine iniquity and the

---

[1] Mírzá Hádí Dawlat-Ábádí, one of the divines of Iṣfahán, who became a follower of the Báb, later supported Mírzá Yaḥyá, and was appointed his representative in Írán and his successor. During the persecutions against the Bábís he recanted his faith.

[2] The insignia of a mullá.

iniquity of such people as thyself have waxed so grievous that the Pen of Glory was moved to make such observations. Fear thou God. He Who heralded this Revelation hath declared: 'He shall proclaim under all conditions: "Verily, verily, I am God, no God is there but Me, the Help in Peril, the Self-Subsisting."'

O people of the Bayán! Ye have been forbidden to contact the loved ones of God. Why hath this ban been imposed and for what purpose? Be ye fair, I adjure you by God, and be not of the heedless. Unto such as are endued with insight, and before the Most Great Beauty, the object of this ban is known and evident; it is so that no one may become aware of his (Hádí's) secrets and deeds.

O Hádí! Thou hast not been in Our company, thou art therefore ignorant of the Cause. Act not according to thine idle imaginings. Aside from these things, scrutinize the Writings with thine own eyes and ponder upon that which hath come to pass. Have pity upon thyself and upon the servants of God and be not the cause of waywardness like unto the people aforetime. The path is unmistakable and the proof is evident. Change injustice into justice and inequity into equity. We cherish the hope that the breaths of divine inspiration may strengthen thee and that thine inner ear may be enabled to hear the blessed words: 'Say, it is God, then leave them to entertain themselves with their cavillings.'[1] Thou hast been there (Cyprus) and hast seen him (Mírzá Yaḥyá). Now speak forth with fairness. Do not misrepresent the matter, neither to thyself nor to the people. Thou art both ignorant and uninformed. Give ear unto the Voice of this Wronged One and hasten towards the ocean of divine knowledge that perchance thou mayest be adorned with the ornament of comprehension and

[1] Qur'án 6:91.

mayest renounce all else but God. Hearken unto the Voice of this benevolent Counsellor, calling aloud, unveiled and manifest, before the faces of kings and their subjects, and summon the people of the world, one and all, unto Him Who is the Lord of Eternity. This is the Word from Whose horizon the day-star of unfailing grace shineth resplendent.

O Hádí! This Wronged One, rid of all attachment to the world, hath striven with utmost endeavour to quench the fire of animosity and hatred which burneth fiercely in the hearts of the peoples of the earth. It behoveth every just and fair-minded person to render thanks unto God—exalted be His glory—and to arise to promote this pre-eminent Cause, that fire may turn into light, and hatred may give way to fellowship and love. I swear by the righteousness of God! This is the sole purpose of this Wronged One. Indeed in proclaiming this momentous Cause and in demonstrating its Truth We have endured manifold sufferings, hardships and tribulations. Thou thyself wouldst bear witness unto that which We have mentioned, couldst thou but speak with fairness. Verily God speaketh the truth and leadeth the Way. He is the Powerful, the Mighty, the Gracious.

May Our Glory rest upon the people of Bahá whom neither the tyranny of the oppressor nor the ascendancy of the aggressor have been able to withhold from God, the Lord of the worlds.

5

TAJALLÍYÁT
(Effulgences)

This is the Epistle of God, the Help in Peril, the Self-Subsisting

He is the One Who heareth from His Realm of Glory.

GOD testifieth that there is none other God but Him and that He Who hath appeared is the Hidden Mystery, the Treasured Symbol, the Most Great Book for all peoples, and the Heaven of bounty for the whole world. He is the Most Mighty Sign amongst men and the Dayspring of the most august attributes in the realm of creation. Through Him hath appeared that which had been hidden from time immemorial and been veiled from the eyes of men. He is the One Whose Manifestation was announced by the heavenly Scriptures, in former times and more recently. Whoso acknowledgeth belief in Him and in His signs and testimonies hath in truth acknowledged that which the Tongue of Grandeur uttered ere the creation of earth and heaven and the revelation of the Kingdom of Names. Through Him the ocean of knowledge hath surged amidst mankind and the river of divine wisdom hath gushed out at the behest of God, the Lord of Days.

Well is it with the man of discernment who hath recognized and perceived the Truth, and the one possessed of a hearing ear who hath hearkened unto His sweet Voice, and the hand that hath received His Book with such resolve as is born of God, the Lord of this world and of the next, and the earnest wayfarer who hath hastened unto His glorious Horizon, and the one endued with strength whom neither the overpowering might of the rulers, nor the tumult raised by the leaders of religion hath been able to shake. And woe betide him who hath rejected the grace of God and His bounty, and hath denied His tender mercy and authority; such a man is indeed reckoned with those who have throughout eternity repudiated the testimony of God and His proof.

Great is the blessedness of him who hath in this Day cast away the things current amongst men and hath clung unto that which is ordained by God, the Lord of Names and the Fashioner of all created things, He Who is come from the heaven of eternity through the power of the Most Great Name, invested with so invincible an authority that all the powers of the earth are unable to withstand Him. Unto this beareth witness the Mother Book, calling from the Most Sublime Station.

O 'Alí-Akbar![1] We have repeatedly heard thy voice and have responded to thee with that which the praise of all mankind can never rival; from which the sincere ones inhale the sweet savours of the sayings of the All-Merciful, and His true lovers perceive the fragrance of heavenly re-union, and the sore athirst discover the murmuring of the water that is life indeed. Blessed the man who hath attained thereto and hath recognized that which is at this moment being diffused from the Pen of God, the Help in Peril, the Almighty, the All-Bountiful.

---

[1] Ustád 'Alí-Akbar, one of the staunch believers in Yazd. He designed the Mashriqu'l-Adhkár of 'Ishqábád and his design was approved by 'Abdu'l-Bahá. Ustád 'Alí-Akbar offered up his life as a martyr in Yazd in 1903.

We testify that thou hast set thy face towards God and travelled far until thou didst attain His presence and gavest ear unto the Voice of this Wronged One, Who hath been cast into prison through the misdeeds of those who have disbelieved in the signs and testimonies of God and have denied this heavenly grace through which the whole world hath been made to shine. Blessed thy face, for it hath turned unto Him, and thine ear, for it hath heard His Voice, and thy tongue, for it hath celebrated the praise of God, the Lord of lords. We pray God to graciously aid thee to become a standard for the promotion of His Cause and to enable thee to draw nigh unto Him at all times and under all conditions.

The chosen ones of God and His loved ones in that land are remembered by Us, and We give them the joyful tidings of that which hath been sent down in their honour from the Kingdom of the utterance of their Lord, the sovereign Ruler of the Day of Reckoning. Make mention of Me to them and illumine them with the resplendent glory of Mine utterance. Verily thy Lord is the Gracious, the Bountiful.

O thou who dost magnify My praise! Give ear unto that which the people of tyranny ascribe unto Me in My days. Some of them say: 'He hath laid claim to divinity'; others say: 'He hath devised a lie against God'; still others say: 'He is come to foment sedition'. Base and wretched are they. Lo! They are, in truth, enslaved to idle imaginings.

We shall now cease using the eloquent language.[1] Truly thy Lord is the Potent, the Unconstrained. We would fain speak in the Persian tongue that perchance the people of Persia, one and all, may become aware of the utterances of the merciful Lord, and come forth to discover the Truth.

[1] Arabic.

The first Tajallí

which hath dawned from the Day-Star of Truth is the knowledge of God—exalted be His glory. And the knowledge of the King of everlasting days can in no wise be attained save by recognizing Him Who is the Bearer of the Most Great Name. He is, in truth, the Speaker on Sinai Who is now seated upon the throne of Revelation. He is the Hidden Mystery and the Treasured Symbol. All the former and latter Books of God are adorned with His praise and extol His glory. Through Him the standard of knowledge hath been planted in the world and the ensign of the oneness of God hath been unfurled amidst all peoples. Attainment unto the Divine Presence can be realized solely by attaining His presence. Through His potency everything that hath, from time immemorial, been veiled and hidden, is now revealed. He is made manifest through the power of Truth and hath uttered a Word whereby all that are in the heavens and on the earth have been dumbfounded, except those whom the Almighty was pleased to exempt. True belief in God and recognition of Him cannot be complete save by acceptance of that which He hath revealed and by observance of whatsoever hath been decreed by Him and set down in the Book by the Pen of Glory.

They that immerse themselves in the ocean of His utterances should at all times have the utmost regard for the divinely-revealed ordinances and prohibitions. Indeed His ordinances constitute the mightiest stronghold for the protection of the world and the safeguarding of its peoples —a light upon those who acknowledge and recognize the truth, and a fire unto such as turn away and deny.

The second Tajallí

is to remain steadfast in the Cause of God—exalted be His glory—and to be unswerving in His love. And this can in no wise be attained except through full recognition of Him; and full recognition cannot be obtained save by faith in the blessed words: 'He doeth whatsoever He willeth.' Whoso tenaciously cleaveth unto this sublime word and drinketh deep from the living waters of utterance which are inherent therein, will be imbued with such a constancy that all the books of the world will be powerless to deter him from the Mother Book. O how glorious is this sublime station, this exalted rank, this ultimate purpose!

O 'Alí-Akbar! Consider how abject is the state of the disbelievers. They all give utterance to the words: 'Verily He is to be praised in His deeds and is to be obeyed in His behest.' Nevertheless if We reveal aught which, even to the extent of a needle's eye, runneth counter to their selfish ways and desires, they will disdainfully reject it. Say, none can ever fathom the manifold exigencies of God's consummate wisdom. In truth, were He to pronounce the earth to be heaven, no one hath the right to question His authority. This is that whereunto the Point of the Bayán hath testified in all that was sent down unto Him with truth at the behest of God, He Who hath caused the Dawn to break.

The third Tajallí

is concerning arts, crafts and sciences. Knowledge is as wings to man's life, and a ladder for his ascent. Its acquisition is incumbent upon everyone. The knowledge of such sciences, however, should be acquired as can profit the peoples of the earth, and not those which begin with words and end with words. Great indeed is the claim of scientists and craftsmen on the peoples of the world. Unto this beareth witness the Mother Book on the day of His return. Happy are those possessed of a hearing ear. In truth, knowledge is a veritable treasure for man, and a source of glory, of bounty, of joy, of exaltation, of cheer and gladness unto him. Thus hath the Tongue of Grandeur spoken in this Most Great Prison.

The fourth Tajallí

is concerning Divinity, Godhead and the like. Were a man of insight to direct his gaze towards the blessed, the manifest Lote-Tree and its fruits, he would be so enriched thereby as to be independent of aught else and to acknowledge his belief in that which the Speaker on Sinai hath uttered from the throne of Revelation.

O 'Alí-Akbar! Acquaint the people with the holy verses of thy Lord and make known unto them His straight Path, His mighty Announcement.

Say: O people, if ye judge fairly and equitably, ye will testify to the truth of whatsoever hath streamed forth from the Most Exalted Pen. If ye be of the people of the Bayán, the Persian Bayán will guide you aright and will prove a sufficient testimony unto you; and if ye be of the people of the Qur'án, ponder ye upon the Revelation on Sinai and the Voice from the Bush which came unto the Son of 'Imrán [Moses].

Gracious God! It was intended that at the time of the manifestation of the One true God the faculty of recognizing Him would have been developed and matured and would have reached its culmination. However, it is now clearly demonstrated that in the disbelievers this faculty hath remained undeveloped and hath, indeed, degenerated.

O 'Alí! That which they accepted from the Bush they now refuse to accept from Him Who is the Tree of the world of existence. Say, O people of the Bayán, speak not according to the dictates of passion and selfish desire. Most of the peoples of the earth attest the truth of the blessed Word which hath come forth from the Bush.

By the righteousness of God! But for the anthem of praise voiced by Him Who heralded the divine Revelation, this Wronged One would never have breathed a word which might have struck terror into the hearts of the ignorant and caused them to perish. Dwelling on the glorification of Him Whom God shall make manifest— exalted be His Manifestation—the Báb in the beginning of the Bayán saith: 'He is the One Who shall proclaim under all conditions, "Verily, verily, I am God, no God is there but Me, the Lord of all created things. In truth all others except Me are My creatures. O, My creatures! Me alone do ye worship."' Likewise in another instance He, magnifying the Name of Him Who shall be made manifest, saith: 'I would be the first to adore Him.' Now it behoveth one to reflect upon the significance of the 'Adorer' and the 'Adored One', that perchance the people of the earth may partake of a dewdrop from the ocean of divine knowledge and may be enabled to perceive the greatness of this Revelation. Verily, He hath appeared and hath unloosed His tongue to proclaim the Truth. Well is it with him who doth acknowledge and recognize the truth, and woe betide the froward and the wayward.

O kindreds of the earth! Incline your ears unto the Voice from the divine Lote-Tree which overshadoweth

the world and be not of the people of tyranny on earth—
men who have repudiated the Manifestation of God and
His invincible authority and have renounced His favours—
they in truth are reckoned with the contemptible in the
Book of God, the Lord of all mankind.

The Glory which hath dawned above the horizon of
My tender mercy rest upon thee and upon whosoever is
with thee and giveth ear to thy words concerning the
Cause of God, the Almighty, the All-Praised.

6

KALIMÁT-I-FIRDAWSÍYYIH

(Words of Paradise)

He is the One Who speaketh through the power of Truth in the Kingdom of Utterance

 YE the embodiments of justice and equity and the manifestations of uprightness and of heavenly bounties! In tears and lamenting, this Wronged One calleth aloud and saith: O God, my God! Adorn the heads of Thy loved ones with the crown of detachment and attire their temples with the raiment of righteousness.

It behoveth the people of Bahá to render the Lord victorious through the power of their utterance and to admonish the people by their goodly deeds and character, inasmuch as deeds exert greater influence than words.

O Ḥaydar-'Alí![1] Upon thee be the praise of God and His glory. Say: Honesty, virtue, wisdom and a saintly character redound to the exaltation of man, while dishonesty, imposture, ignorance and hypocrisy lead to his abasement. By My life! Man's distinction lieth not in ornaments or wealth, but rather in virtuous behaviour and true understanding. Most of the people in Persia are steeped in deception and idle fancy. How great the difference between the condition of these people and the station

---

[1] Ḥájí Mírzá Ḥaydar-'Alí, outstanding Persian Bahá'í teacher and author. He spent nine years in prison and exile in Khartúm, travelled extensively in Írán, and passed away in 1920 in the Holy Land. Western pilgrims knew him as the Angel of Mount Carmel.

of such valiant souls as have passed beyond the sea of names and pitched their tents upon the shores of the ocean of detachment. Indeed none but a few of the existing generation hath yet earned the merit of hearkening unto the warblings of the doves of the all-highest Paradise. 'Few of My servants are truly thankful.'[1] People for the most part delight in superstitions. They regard a single drop of the sea of delusion as preferable to an ocean of certitude. By holding fast unto names they deprive themselves of the inner reality and by clinging to vain imaginings they are kept back from the Dayspring of heavenly signs. God grant you may be graciously aided under all conditions to shatter the idols of superstition and to tear away the veils of the imaginations of men. Authority lieth in the grasp of God, the Fountainhead of revelation and inspiration and the Lord of the Day of Resurrection.

We heard that which the person in question hath mentioned regarding certain teachers of the Faith. Indeed he hath spoken truly. Some heedless souls roam the lands in the name of God, actively engaged in ruining His Cause, and call it promoting and teaching the Word of God; and this notwithstanding that the qualifications of the teachers of the Faith, like unto stars, shine resplendent throughout the heavens of the divine Tablets. Every fair-minded person testifieth and every man of insight is well aware that the One true God—exalted be His glory—hath unceasingly set forth and expounded that which will elevate the station and will exalt the rank of the children of men.

The people of Bahá burn brightly amidst the gatherings even as a candle and hold fast unto that which God hath purposed. This station standeth supreme above all stations. Well is it with him who hath cast away the things that the

1 Qur'án 34:12.

people of the world possess, yearning for that which pertaineth unto God, the Sovereign Lord of eternity.

Say: O God, my God! Thou beholdest me circling round Thy Will with mine eyes turned towards the horizon of Thy bounty, eagerly awaiting the revelation of the effulgent splendours of the sun of Thy favours. I beg of Thee, O Beloved of every understanding heart and the Desire of such as have near access unto Thee, to grant that Thy loved ones may become wholly detached from their own inclinations, holding fast unto that which pleaseth Thee. Attire them, O Lord, with the robe of righteousness and illumine them with the splendours of the light of detachment. Summon then to their assistance the hosts of wisdom and utterance that they may exalt Thy Word amongst Thy creatures and proclaim Thy Cause amidst Thy servants. Verily, potent art Thou to do what Thou willest, and within Thy grasp lie the reins of all affairs. No God is there but Thee, the Mighty, the Ever-Forgiving.

O thou who hast turned thy gaze towards My face! In these days there occurred that which hath plunged Me into dire sadness. Certain wrong-doers who profess allegiance to the Cause of God committed such deeds as have caused the limbs of sincerity, of honesty, of justice, of equity to quake. One known individual to whom the utmost kindness and favour had been extended perpetrated such acts as have brought tears to the eye of God. Formerly We uttered words of warning and premonition, then for a number of years We kept the matter secret that haply he might take heed and repent. But all to no purpose. In the end he bent his energies upon vilifying the Cause of God before the eyes of all men. He tore the veil of fairness asunder and felt sympathy neither for himself nor for the Cause of God. Now, however, the deeds of certain individuals have brought sorrows far more grievous than those which the deeds of the former had caused. Beseech thou God, the True One, that He may graciously enable the heedless to retract and repent. Verily He is the Forgiving, the Bountiful, the Most Generous.

In these days it is incumbent upon everyone to adhere tenaciously unto unity and concord and to labour diligently in promoting the Cause of God, that perchance the wayward souls may attain that which will lead unto abiding prosperity.

In brief, dissensions among various sects have opened the way to weakness. Each sect hath picked out a way for itself and is clinging to a certain cord. Despite manifest blindness and ignorance they pride themselves on their insight and knowledge. Among them are mystics who bear allegiance to the Faith of Islám, some of whom indulge in that which leadeth to idleness and seclusion. I swear by God! It lowereth man's station and maketh him swell with pride. Man must bring forth fruit. One who yieldeth no fruit is, in the words of the Spirit,[1] like unto a fruitless tree, and a fruitless tree is fit but for the fire.

That which the aforesaid persons have mentioned concerning the stations of Divine Unity will conduce in no small measure to idleness and vain imaginings. These mortal men have evidently set aside the differences of station and have come to regard themselves as God, while God is immeasurably exalted above all things. Every created being however revealeth His signs which are but emanations from Him and not His Own Self. All these signs are reflected and can be seen in the book of existence, and the scrolls that depict the shape and pattern of the universe are indeed a most great book. Therein every man

[1] Jesus.

of insight can perceive that which would lead to the Straight Path and would enable him to attain the Great Announcement. Consider the rays of the sun whose light hath encompassed the world. The rays emanate from the sun and reveal its nature, but are not the sun itself. Whatsoever can be discerned on earth amply demonstrateth the power of God, His knowledge and the outpourings of His bounty, while He Himself is immeasurably exalted above all creatures.

Christ saith: 'Thou hast granted to children that whereof the learned and the wise are deprived.' The sage of Sabzivár[1] hath said: 'Alas! Attentive ears are lacking, otherwise the whisperings of the Sinaic Bush could be heard from every tree.' In a Tablet to a man of wisdom who had made enquiry as to the meaning of Elementary Reality, We addressed this famous sage in these words: 'If this saying is truly thine, how is it that thou hast failed to hearken unto the Call which the Tree of Man hath raised from the loftiest heights of the world? If thou didst hear the Call yet fear and the desire to preserve thy life prompted thee to remain heedless to it, thou art such a person as hath never been nor is worthy of mention; if thou hast not heard it, then thou art bereft of the sense of hearing.' In brief, such men are they whose words are the pride of the world, and whose deeds are the shame of the nations.

Verily We have sounded the Trumpet which is none other than My Pen of Glory, and lo, mankind hath swooned away before it, save them whom God pleaseth to deliver as a token of His grace. He is the Lord of bounty, the Ancient of Days.

Say: O concourse of divines! Pronounce ye censure

---

[1] Ḥájí Mullá Hádí Sabzivárí, a renowned philosopher and poet of Írán contemporary with Bahá'u'lláh. He passed away in 1873.

against this Pen unto which, as soon as it raised its shrill voice, the kingdom of utterance prepared itself to hearken, and before whose mighty and glorious theme every other theme hath paled into insignificance? Fear ye God and follow not your idle fancies and corrupt imaginings, but rather follow Him Who is come unto you invested with undeniable knowledge and unshakeable certitude.

Glorified be God! Man's treasure is his utterance, yet this Wronged One hath withheld His Tongue, for the disbelievers are lying in ambush; however, protection is afforded by God, the Lord of all worlds. Verily, in Him have We placed Our trust and unto Him have We committed all affairs. All-Sufficient is He for Us and for all created things. He is the One by Whose leave, and through the potency of Whose command, the Day-Star of sovereign might hath shone resplendent above the horizon of the world. Well is it with him who perceiveth and recognizeth the Truth and woe betide the froward and the faithless.

This Wronged One hath invariably treated the wise with affection. By the wise is meant men whose knowledge is not confined to mere words and whose lives have been fruitful and have produced enduring results. It is incumbent upon everyone to honour these blessed souls. Happy are they that observe God's precepts; happy are they that have recognized the Truth; happy are they that judge with fairness in all matters and hold fast to the Cord of My inviolable Justice.

The people of Persia have turned away from Him Who is the Protector and the Helper. They are clinging to and have enmeshed themselves in the vain imaginings of the foolish. So firmly do they adhere to superstitions that naught can sever them therefrom save the potent arm of God—exalted is His glory. Beseech thou the Almighty that

He may remove with the fingers of divine power the veils which have shut out the divers peoples and kindreds, that they may attain the things that are conducive to security, progress and advancement and may hasten forth towards the incomparable Friend.

The word of God which the Abhá Pen hath revealed and inscribed on the

first leaf

of the Most Exalted Paradise is this: Verily I say: The fear of God hath ever been a sure defence and a safe stronghold for all the peoples of the world. It is the chief cause of the protection of mankind, and the supreme instrument for its preservation. Indeed, there existeth in man a faculty which deterreth him from, and guardeth him against, whatever is unworthy and unseemly, and which is known as his sense of shame. This, however, is confined to but a few; all have not possessed and do not possess it.

The word of God which the Supreme Pen hath recorded on the

second leaf

of the Most Exalted Paradise is the following: The Pen of the Most High exhorteth, at this moment, the manifestations of authority and the sources of power, namely the kings, the sovereigns, the presidents, the rulers, the divines and the wise, and enjoineth them to uphold the cause of religion, and to cleave unto it. Religion is verily the chief instrument for the establishment of order in the world and of tranquillity amongst its peoples. The weakening of the pillars of religion hath strengthened the foolish and emboldened them and made them more arrogant. Verily I say: The greater the decline of religion, the more grievous the waywardness of the ungodly. This cannot but lead in the end to chaos and confusion. Hear Me, O men of insight, and be warned, ye who are endued with discernment!

The word of God which the Supreme Pen hath recorded on the

third leaf

of the Most Exalted Paradise is this: O son of man! If thine eyes be turned towards mercy, forsake the things that profit thee and cleave unto that which will profit mankind. And if thine eyes be turned towards justice, choose thou for thy neighbour that which thou choosest for thyself. Humility exalteth man to the heaven of glory and power, whilst pride abaseth him to the depths of wretchedness and degradation.

O people of God! Great is the Day and mighty the Call! In one of Our Tablets We have revealed these exalted words: 'Were the world of the spirit to be wholly converted into the sense of hearing, it could then claim to be worthy to hearken unto the Voice that calleth from the Supreme Horizon; for otherwise, these ears that are defiled with lying tales have never been, nor are they now, fit to hear it.' Well is it with them that hearken; and woe betide the wayward.

The word of God which the Supreme Pen hath recorded
on the

fourth leaf

of the Most Exalted Paradise is the following: O people of
God! Beseech ye the True One—glorified be His Name—
that He may graciously shield the manifestations of
dominion and power from the suggestions of self and
desire and shed the radiance of justice and guidance upon
them.

His Majesty Muḥammad S͟háh, despite the excellence of
his rank, committed two heinous deeds. One was the order
to banish the Lord of the Realms of Grace and Bounty, the
Primal Point; and the other, the murder of the Prince of the
City of Statesmanship and Literary Accomplishment.[1]

The faults of kings, like their favours, can be great. A
king who is not deterred by the vainglory of power and
authority from observing justice, nor is deprived of the
splendours of the day-star of equity by luxury, riches, glory
or the marshalling of hosts and legions shall occupy a high
rank and a sublime station amongst the Concourse on high.
It is incumbent upon everyone to extend aid and to manifest kindness to so noble a soul. Well is it with the king who
keepeth a tight hold on the reins of his passion, restraineth
his anger and preferreth justice and fairness to injustice and
tyranny.

---

[1] Mírzá Abu'l-Qásim Faráhání, the Qá'im Maqám, a distinguished
poet and scholar during the reign of Fatḥ 'Alí S͟háh. He was a
friend of Mírzá Buzurg, father of Bahá'u'lláh. Qá'im Maqám
became Prime Minister of Persia in 1821, but in 1835 he was put
to death by order of Muḥammad S͟háh, at the instigation of Ḥájí
Mírzá Áqásí.

The word of God which the Supreme Pen hath recorded on the

fifth leaf

of the Most Exalted Paradise is this: Above all else, the greatest gift and the most wondrous blessing hath ever been and will continue to be Wisdom. It is man's unfailing Protector. It aideth him and strengtheneth him. Wisdom is God's Emissary and the Revealer of His Name the Omniscient. Through it the loftiness of man's station is made manifest and evident. It is all-knowing and the foremost Teacher in the school of existence. It is the Guide and is invested with high distinction. Thanks to its educating influence earthly beings have become imbued with a gemlike spirit which outshineth the heavens. In the city of justice it is the unrivalled Speaker Who, in the year nine, illumined the world with the joyful tidings of this Revelation. And it was this peerless Source of wisdom that at the beginning of the foundation of the world ascended the stair of inner meaning and when enthroned upon the pulpit of utterance, through the operation of the divine Will, proclaimed two words. The first heralded the promise of reward, while the second voiced the ominous warning of punishment. The promise gave rise to hope and the warning begat fear. Thus the basis of world order hath been firmly established upon these twin principles. Exalted is the Lord of Wisdom, the Possessor of Great Bounty.

The word of God which the Supreme Pen hath recorded on the

sixth leaf

of the Most Exalted Paradise is the following: The light of

men is Justice. Quench it not with the contrary winds of oppression and tyranny. The purpose of justice is the appearance of unity among men. The ocean of divine wisdom surgeth within this exalted word, while the books of the world cannot contain its inner significance. Were mankind to be adorned with this raiment, they would behold the day-star of the utterance, 'On that day God will satisfy everyone out of His abundance,'[1] shining resplendent above the horizon of the world. Appreciate ye the value of this utterance; it is a noble fruit that the Tree of the Pen of Glory hath yielded. Happy is the man that giveth ear unto it and observeth its precepts. Verily I say, whatever is sent down from the heaven of the Will of God is the means for the establishment of order in the world and the instrument for promoting unity and fellowship among its peoples. Thus hath the Tongue of this Wronged One spoken from His Most Great Prison.

The word of God which the Supreme Pen hath recorded on the

seventh leaf

of the Most Exalted Paradise is this: O ye men of wisdom among nations! Shut your eyes to estrangement, then fix your gaze upon unity. Cleave tenaciously unto that which will lead to the well-being and tranquillity of all mankind. This span of earth is but one homeland and one habitation. It behoveth you to abandon vainglory which causeth alienation and to set your hearts on whatever will ensure

[1] cf. Qur'án 4:129.

harmony. In the estimation of the people of Bahá man's glory lieth in his knowledge, his upright conduct, his praiseworthy character, his wisdom, and not in his nationality or rank. O people of the earth! Appreciate the value of this heavenly word. Indeed it may be likened unto a ship for the ocean of knowledge and a shining luminary for the realm of perception.

The word of God which the Supreme Pen hath recorded on the

eighth leaf

of the Most Exalted Paradise is the following: Schools must first train the children in the principles of religion, so that the Promise and the Threat recorded in the Books of God may prevent them from the things forbidden and adorn them with the mantle of the commandments; but this in such a measure that it may not injure the children by resulting in ignorant fanaticism and bigotry.

It is incumbent upon the Trustees of the House of Justice to take counsel together regarding those things which have not outwardly been revealed in the Book, and to enforce that which is agreeable to them. God will verily inspire them with whatsoever He willeth, and He, verily, is the Provider, the Omniscient.

We have formerly ordained that people should converse in two languages, yet efforts must be made to reduce them to one, likewise the scripts of the world, that men's lives may not be dissipated and wasted in learning divers languages. Thus the whole earth would come to be regarded as one city and one land.

The word of God which the Supreme Pen hath recorded on the

ninth leaf

of the Most Exalted Paradise is this: In all matters modera-tion is desirable. If a thing is carried to excess, it will prove a source of evil. Consider the civilization of the West, how it hath agitated and alarmed the peoples of the world. An infernal engine hath been devised, and hath proved so cruel a weapon of destruction that its like none hath ever witnes-sed or heard. The purging of such deeply-rooted and overwhelming corruptions cannot be effected unless the peoples of the world unite in pursuit of one common aim and embrace one universal faith. Incline your ears unto the Call of this Wronged One and adhere firmly to the Lesser Peace.

Strange and astonishing things exist in the earth but they are hidden from the minds and the understanding of men. These things are capable of changing the whole atmosphere of the earth and their contamination would prove lethal. Great God! We have observed an amazing thing. Lightning or a force similar to it is controlled by an operator and moveth at his command. Immeasurably exalted is the Lord of Power Who hath laid bare that which He purposed through the potency of His weighty and invincible com-mand.

O people of Bahá! Each one of the ordinances We have revealed is a mighty stronghold for the preservation of the world of being. Verily, this Wronged One desireth naught but your security and elevation.

We exhort the men of the House of Justice and com-mand them to ensure the protection and safeguarding of men, women and children. It is incumbent upon them to have the utmost regard for the interests of the people at all times and under all conditions. Blessed is the ruler who succoureth the captive, and the rich one who careth for the poor, and the just one who secureth from the wrong doer the rights of the downtrodden, and happy the trustee who observeth that which the Ordainer, the Ancient of Days hath prescribed unto him.

O Ḥaydar-'Alí! Upon thee be My glory and My praise. My counsels and admonitions have compassed the world. Yet, instead of imparting joy and gladness they have caused grief, because some of those who claim to love Me have waxed haughty and have inflicted upon Me such tribulations as neither the followers of former religions nor the divines of Persia did ever inflict.

We have said: 'My imprisonment doeth Me no harm, nor do the things that have befallen Me at the hands of My enemies. That which harmeth Me is the conduct of my loved ones who, though they bear My name, yet commit that which maketh My heart and My pen to lament.' Such utterances as these have again and again been revealed, yet the heedless have failed to profit thereby, since they are captive to their own evil passions and corrupt desires. Beseech thou the One true God that He may enable everyone to repent and return unto Him. So long as one's nature yieldeth unto evil passions, crime and transgression will prevail. We cherish the hope that the hand of divine power and the outpouring of heavenly blessings may sustain all men, may attire them with the vesture of forgiveness and bounty and guard them against that which would harm His Cause among His servants. He is, in truth, the Potent, the All-Powerful, and He is the Ever-Forgiving, the Merciful.

The word of God which the Supreme Pen hath recorded on the

tenth leaf

of the Most Exalted Paradise is the following: O people of the earth! Living in seclusion or practising asceticism is not acceptable in the presence of God. It behoveth them that are endued with insight and understanding to observe that which will cause joy and radiance. Such practices as are sprung from the loins of idle fancy or are begotten of the womb of superstition ill beseem men of knowledge. In former times and more recently some people have been taking up their abodes in the caves of the mountains while others have repaired to graveyards at night. Say, give ear unto the counsels of this Wronged One. Abandon the things current amongst you and adopt that which the faithful Counsellor biddeth you. Deprive not yourselves of the bounties which have been created for your sake.

Charity is pleasing and praiseworthy in the sight of God and is regarded as a prince among goodly deeds. Consider ye and call to mind that which the All-Merciful hath revealed in the Qur'án: 'They prefer them before themselves, though poverty be their own lot. And with such as are preserved from their own covetousness shall it be well.'[1] Viewed in this light, the blessed utterance above is, in truth, the day-star of utterances. Blessed is he who preferreth his brother before himself. Verily, such a man is reckoned, by virtue of the Will of God, the All-Knowing, the All-Wise, with the people of Bahá who dwell in the Crimson Ark.

[1] Qur'án 59:9.

The word of God which the Supreme Pen hath recorded on the

eleventh leaf

of the Most Exalted Paradise is this: We enjoin upon them that are the emblems of His names and attributes to firmly adhere henceforth unto that which hath been set forth in this Most Great Revelation, not to allow themselves to become the cause of strife, and, until the end that knoweth no end, to keep their eyes directed towards the dayspring of these resplendent words which have been recorded in this Tablet. Strife leads to bloodshed and provokes commotion amongst people. Hearken ye unto the Voice of this Wronged One and deviate not therefrom.

Were anyone to ponder in his heart that which hath, in this Revelation, streamed forth from the Pen of Glory, he would be assured that whatever this Wronged One hath affirmed He hath had no intention of establishing any position or distinction for Himself. The purpose hath rather been to attract the souls, through the sublimity of His words, unto the summit of transcendent glory and to endow them with the capacity of perceiving that which will purge and purify the peoples of the world from the strife and dissension which religious differences provoke. Unto this bear witness My heart, My Pen, My inner and My outer Being. God grant that all men may turn unto the treasuries latent within their own beings.

O people of Bahá! The source of crafts, sciences and arts is the power of reflection. Make ye every effort that out of this ideal mine there may gleam forth such pearls of wisdom and utterance as will promote the well-being and harmony of all the kindreds of the earth.

Under all conditions, whether in adversity or at ease,

whether honoured or afflicted, this Wronged One hath directed all men to show forth love, affection, compassion and harmony. And yet whenever there was any slight evidence of progress and advancement, those concealed behind the veils would sally forth and utter calumnies more wounding than the sword. They cling unto misleading and reprehensible words and suffer themselves to be deprived of the ocean of verses revealed by God.

If these obstructing veils had not intervened Persia would, in some two years, have been subdued through the power of utterance, the position of both the government and the people would have been raised and the Supreme Goal, unveiled and unconcealed, would have appeared in the plenitude of glory. In short, sometimes in explicit language, at other times by allusion, We said whatever had to be said. Thus, once Persia had been rehabilitated, the sweet savours of the Word of God would have wafted over all countries, inasmuch as that which hath streamed forth from the Most Exalted Pen is conducive to the glory, the advancement and education of all the peoples and kindreds of the earth. Indeed it is the sovereign remedy for every disease, could they but comprehend and perceive it.

Recently the Afnáns and Amín—upon them be My glory and loving-kindness—attained Our presence and beheld Our countenance; likewise Nabíl, the son of Nabíl and the son of Samandar—upon them rest the glory of God and His loving-kindness—are present and have drunk the cup of reunion. We entreat God that He may graciously ordain for them the good of this world and of the next and that the outpouring of His blessings and grace may descend upon them from the heaven of His generosity and the clouds of His tender compassion. Verily of those who show mercy He is the Most Merciful, and He is the Gracious, the Beneficent.

O Ḥaydar-'Alí! Thine other letter which thou hadst forwarded through him who beareth the title of Júd[1] (Bounty) hath reached Our holy court. Praised be God! It was adorned with the light of divine unity and of detachment and was ablaze with the fire of love and affection. Pray thou unto God that He may grant keenness to the eyes and illumine them with a new light, perchance they may perceive that which hath no parallel nor peer.

In this day the verses of the Mother Book are resplendent and unmistakable even as the sun. They can in no wise be mistaken for any of the past or more recent utterances. Truly this Wronged One desireth not to demonstrate His Own Cause with proofs produced by others. He is the One Who embraceth all things, while all else besides Him is circumscribed. Say, O people, peruse that which is current amongst you and We will peruse what pertaineth unto Us. I swear by God! Neither the praise of the peoples of the world, nor the things that the kindreds of the earth possess are worthy of mention before the remembrance of His Name. Unto this beareth witness He Who under all conditions proclaimeth, 'Verily He is God, the sovereign Ruler of the Day of Reckoning and the Lord of the mighty Throne.'

Glorified be God! One wondereth by what proof or reason the disbelievers among the people of the Bayán have turned away from the Lord of being. In truth the station of

---

[1] Muḥammad Javád-i-Qazvíní, upon whom Bahá'u'lláh bestowed the title Ismu'lláhi'l-Júd (The Name of God, Bounty). He transcribed numerous Tablets of Bahá'u'lláh during His Ministry, but subsequently broke the Covenant. (See *God Passes By* pages 247 and 319.)

this Revelation transcendeth the station of whatever hath been manifested in the past or will be made manifest in the future.

Were the Point of the Bayán present in this day and should He, God forbid, hesitate to acknowledge this Cause, then the very blessed words which have streamed forth from the wellspring of His Own Bayán would apply to Him. He saith, and His word is the truth, 'Lawful is it for Him Whom God will make manifest to reject him who is the greatest on earth.' Say, O ye that are bereft of understanding! Today that Most Exalted Being is proclaiming: 'Verily, verily, I am the first to adore Him.' How shallow is the fund of men's knowledge and how feeble their power of perception. Our Pen of Glory beareth witness to their abject poverty and to the wealth of God, the Lord of all worlds.

Lauded and glorified is He Who hath called the creation into being. He is the sovereign Truth, the Knower of things unseen. The Mother Book is revealed and the Lord of Bounty is established upon the most blessed seat of glory. The Dawn hath broken, yet the people understand not. The signs have been ushered in, while He Who hath revealed them is overwhelmed with manifest sorrow. Indeed I have endured that which hath caused the world of existence to lament.

Say: O Yaḥyá (Azal), produce a single verse, if thou dost possess divinely-inspired knowledge. These words were formerly spoken by My Herald Who at this hour proclaimeth: 'Verily, verily, I am the first to adore Him.' Be fair, O My brother. Art thou able to express thyself when brought face to face with the billowing ocean of Mine utterance? Canst thou unloose thy tongue when confronted with the shrill voice of My Pen? Hast thou any power before the revelations of Mine omnipotence? Judge thou fairly, I adjure thee by God, and call to mind when thou didst stand in the presence of this Wronged One and We dictated to thee the verses of God, the Help in Peril, the Self-Subsisting. Beware lest the source of falsehood withhold thee from the manifest Truth.

O thou who hast fixed thy gaze upon My countenance! Say: O ye heedless ones! By reason of a droplet ye have deprived yourselves of the ocean of heavenly verses and for the sake of an insignificant atom ye have shut yourselves out from the splendours of the Day-Star of Truth. Who else but Bahá hath the power to speak forth before the face of mankind? Judge ye fairly and be not of the unjust. Through Him the oceans have surged, the mysteries have been divulged and the trees have lifted up their voices exclaiming: The kingdoms of earth and heaven are God's, the Revealer of signs, the Fountainhead of clear tokens. Peruse ye the Persian Bayán revealed by Him Who heralded this Revelation and look at it with the eye of fairness. Verily He will guide you aright to His Path. At this moment He proclaimeth that which His tongue had formerly uttered when He was seated upon the throne of His most exalted Name.

Thou hast made mention of the loved ones in those regions. Praised be God, each one of them attained the honour of being remembered by the True One—exalted is His glory—and the names of them, one and all, flowed from the Tongue of Grandeur in the kingdom of utterance. Great indeed is their blessedness and happiness, inasmuch as they have drunk the choice wine of revelation and inspiration from the hand of their Lord, the Compassionate, the Merciful. We beseech God to strengthen them to manifest inflexible constancy and to summon to their aid the hosts of wisdom and utterance. He is in truth the Mighty, the Omnipotent. Convey my greetings to them and give them the joyful tidings that the Day-Star of remembrance hath dawned and shed its radiance from above the horizon of the bountiful favours of their Lord, the Ever-Forgiving, the All-Merciful.

Thou hast mentioned Ḥusayn. We have attired his temple with the robe of forgiveness and adorned his head with the crown of pardon. It beseemeth him to pride himself among all men upon this resplendent, this radiant and manifest bounty. Say: Be not despondent. After the revelation of this blessed verse it is as though thou hast been born anew from thy mother's womb. Say: Thou art free from sin and error. Truly God hath purged thee with the living waters of His utterance in His Most Great Prison. We entreat Him—blessed and exalted is He—to graciously confirm thee in extolling Him and in magnifying His glory and to strengthen thee through the power of His invisible hosts. Verily, He is the Almighty, the Omnipotent.

Thou hast made mention of the people of Tár.[1] We have set Our face toward the servants of God therein and advise them first to consider that which the Point of the Bayán hath revealed concerning this Revelation whereby all names and titles have been shaken, the idols of vain imaginings have crumbled and the Tongue of Grandeur hath, from the realm of glory, proclaimed: By the righteousness of God! The Hidden Treasure, the Impenetrable Mystery, hath been uncovered to men's eyes, causing all things, whether of the past or of the future, to rejoice. He hath said, and His word is the truth: 'Of all the tributes I have paid to Him Who is to come after Me, the greatest is this, My written confession, that no words of Mine can adequately describe

[1] A village near Iṣfáhán.

Him, nor can any reference to Him in My Book, the Bayán, do justice to His Cause.'

Moreover We counsel them to observe justice, equity, honesty, piety and that whereby both the Word of God and their own station will be exalted amongst men. Verily I am the One Who exhorteth with justice. Unto this beareth witness He from Whose Pen rivers of mercy have flowed and from Whose utterance fountains of living waters have streamed forth unto all created things. Immeasurably exalted is this boundless grace; immensely blessed is this resplendent favour.

O people of Tár! Give ear unto the Call of Him Who doeth whatsoever He willeth. In truth He remindeth you of that which will draw you nigh unto God, the Lord of the worlds. He hath turned His face towards you from the Prison of 'Akká and hath revealed for your sakes what will immortalize your memory and your names in the Book which cannot be effaced and remaineth unaffected by the doubts of the froward. Cast away the things current amongst men and take fast hold on that whereunto ye are bidden by virtue of the Will of the Ordainer, the Ancient of Days. This is the Day wherein the divine Lote-Tree calleth aloud, saying: O people! Behold ye My fruits and My leaves, incline then your ears unto My rustling. Beware lest the doubts of men debar you from the light of certitude. The Ocean of utterance exclaimeth and saith: 'O ye dwellers on the earth! Behold My billowing waters and the pearls of wisdom and utterance which I have poured forth. Fear ye God and be not of the heedless.'

In this Day a great festival is taking place in the Realm above; for whatsoever was promised in the sacred Scriptures hath been fulfilled. This is the Day of great rejoicing. It behoveth everyone to hasten towards the court of His nearness with exceeding joy, gladness, exultation and delight and to deliver himself from the fire of remoteness.

O people of Tár! Through the strengthening power of My Name seize ye the chalice of knowledge, drink then your fill in defiance of the people of the world who have broken the Covenant of God and His Testament, rejected His proofs and clear tokens, and cavilled at His signs which have pervaded all that are in heaven and on earth.

The disbelievers among the people of the Bayán are like the followers of the Shí'ih sect and walk in their footsteps. Leave them to their idle fancies and vain imaginings. They are in truth accounted with the lost in the Book of God, the All-Knowing, the All-Wise. The Shí'ih divines, one and all, are now engaged in reviling and denouncing the True One from their pulpits. Gracious God! Dawlat-Ábádí[1] too hath followed suit. He ascended the pulpit and gave voice to that which hath caused the Tablet to cry out in anguish and the Pen to wail. Meditate upon his conduct and the conduct of Ashraf[2]—upon him be My glory and My tender mercy—and likewise consider those loved ones who hastened to the place of martyrdom in My Name, and offered up their lives in the path of Him Who is the Desire of the world.

The Cause is manifest, it shineth resplendent as the sun, but the people have become veils unto themselves. We entreat God that He may graciously assist them to return unto Him. He is, in truth, the Forgiving, the Merciful.

O people of Tár! We send you greetings from this Spot and beseech God—blessed and exalted is He—to give you to drink the choice wine of constancy from the hand of

---

[1] See footnote 1 on page 42.

[2] Mírzá Ashraf, who was martyred in the city of Iṣfahán. (See *God Passes By* p. 201.)

His favour. Verily, He is the Lord of Bounty, the Gracious, the All-Praised. Leave ye unto themselves the immature ones of the world—they that are moved by selfish desire and cling to the exponents of idle fancy. Verily He is your Helper and Succourer. He is, in truth, potent to do whatsoever He willeth. No God is there but Him, the One, the Peerless, the Mighty, the Most Great.

May glory from Our presence rest upon those who have set their faces toward the Dayspring of His Revelation and have acknowledged and recognized that which the Tongue of utterance hath spoken in the kingdom of knowledge in this blessed, this glorious and incomparable Day.

7

LAWḤ-I-DUNYÁ
(Tablet of the World)

*In My Name, calling aloud in the Kingdom
of Utterance*

PRAISE and thanksgiving beseem the Lord of
manifest dominion Who hath adorned the
mighty prison with the presence of their honours
'Alí-Akbar and Amín, and hath illumined it
with the light of certitude, constancy and assurance.[1] The
glory of God and the glory of all that are in the heavens
and on the earth be upon them.

Light and glory, greeting and praise be upon the Hands
of His Cause, through whom the light of fortitude hath
shone forth and the truth hath been established that the
authority to choose rests with God, the Powerful, the
Mighty, the Unconstrained, through whom the ocean of
bounty hath surged and the fragrance of the gracious
favours of God, the Lord of mankind, hath been diffused.
We beseech Him—exalted is He—to shield them through
the power of His hosts, to protect them through the
potency of His dominion and to aid them through His
indomitable strength which prevaileth over all created
things. Sovereignty is God's, the Creator of the heavens
and the Lord of the Kingdom of Names.

[1] The two Hands of the Cause of God, Ḥájí Mullá 'Alí-Akbar
Shahmírzádí and Ḥájí Abu'l-Ḥasan Ardakání, Amín-i-Iláhí
(Trustee of Ḥuqúqu'lláh), were originally arrested in Ṭihrán,
imprisoned in Qazvín in the year 1891, and then transferred to
prison in Ṭihrán.

The Great Announcement proclaimeth: O people of Persia! In former times ye have been the symbols of mercy and the embodiments of affection and kindliness. The regions of the world were illumined and embellished by the brightness of the light of your knowledge and by the blaze of your erudition. How is it that you have arisen to destroy yourselves and your friends with your own hands?

O Afnán, O thou that hast branched from Mine ancient Stock! My glory and My loving-kindness rest upon thee. How vast is the tabernacle of the Cause of God! It hath overshadowed all the peoples and kindreds of the earth, and will, ere long, gather together the whole of mankind beneath its shelter. Thy day of service is now come. Countless Tablets bear the testimony of the bounties vouchsafed unto thee. Arise for the triumph of My Cause, and, through the power of thine utterance, subdue the hearts of men. Thou must show forth that which will ensure the peace and the well-being of the miserable and the downtrodden. Gird up the loins of thine endeavour, that perchance thou mayest release the captive from his chains, and enable him to attain unto true liberty.

Justice is, in this day, bewailing its plight, and Equity groaneth beneath the yoke of oppression. The thick clouds of tyranny have darkened the face of the earth, and enveloped its peoples. Through the movement of Our Pen of glory We have, at the bidding of the omnipotent Ordainer, breathed a new life into every human frame, and instilled into every word a fresh potency. All created things proclaim the evidences of this world-wide regeneration. This is the most great, the most joyful tidings imparted by the Pen of this Wronged One to mankind. Wherefore fear ye, O My well-beloved ones? Who is it that can dismay you? A touch of moisture sufficeth to dissolve the hardened clay out of which this perverse generation is moulded. The mere act of your gathering together is enough to scatter the forces of these vain and worthless people.

Strife and conflict befit the beasts of the wild. It was through the grace of God and with the aid of seemly words and praiseworthy deeds that the unsheathed swords of the Bábí community were returned to their scabbards. Indeed through the power of good words, the righteous have always succeeded in winning command over the meads of the hearts of men. Say, O ye loved ones! Do not forsake prudence. Incline your hearts to the counsels given by the Most Exalted Pen and beware lest your hands or tongues cause harm unto anyone among mankind.

Referring to the land of Ṭá [Ṭihrán] We have revealed in the *Kitáb-i-Aqdas* that which will admonish mankind. They that perpetrate tyranny in the world have usurped the rights of the peoples and kindreds of the earth and are sedulously pursuing their selfish inclinations. The tyrant[1] of the land of Yá [Yazd], committed that which hath caused the Concourse on High to shed tears of blood.

O thou who hast quaffed from the wine of Mine utterance and hast fixed thy gaze upon the horizon of My Revelation! How strange that the people of Persia, who were unrivalled in sciences and arts, should have sunk to the lowest level of degradation among the kindreds of the earth. O people! In this blessed, this glorious Day, deprive not yourselves of the liberal effusions of bounty which the Lord of abounding grace hath vouchsafed unto you. In this Day showers of wisdom and utterance are pouring down from the clouds of divine mercy. Well is it with them who judge His Cause with fairness, and woe betide the unjust.

[1] Prince Maḥmúd Mírzá, the Jalálu'd'Dawlih, Governor of Yazd, Persia.

Every man of insight will, in this day, readily admit that the counsels which the Pen of this Wronged One hath revealed constitute the supreme animating power for the advancement of the world and the exaltation of its peoples. Arise, O people, and, by the power of God's might, resolve to gain the victory over your own selves, that haply the whole earth may be freed and sanctified from its servitude to the gods of its idle fancies—gods that have inflicted such loss upon, and are responsible for the misery of their wretched worshippers. These idols form the obstacle that impedeth man in his efforts to advance in the path of perfection. We cherish the hope that the Hand of divine power may lend its assistance to mankind and deliver it from its state of grievous abasement.

In one of the Tablets these words have been revealed: O people of God! Do not busy yourselves in your own concerns; let your thoughts be fixed upon that which will rehabilitate the fortunes of mankind and sanctify the hearts and souls of men. This can best be achieved through pure and holy deeds, through a virtuous life and a goodly behaviour. Valiant acts will ensure the triumph of this Cause, and a saintly character will reinforce its power. Cleave unto righteousness, O people of Bahá! This, verily, is the commandment which this Wronged One hath given unto you, and the first choice of His unrestrained Will for every one of you.

O friends! It behoveth you to refresh and revive your souls through the gracious favours which in this Divine, this soul-stirring Springtime are being showered upon you. The Day-Star of His great glory hath shed its radiance upon you, and the clouds of His limitless grace have overshadowed you. How high the reward of him that hath not deprived himself of so great a bounty, nor failed to recognize the beauty of his Best-Beloved in this, His new attire. Watch over yourselves, for the Evil One is lying in wait, ready to entrap you. Gird yourselves against his wicked devices, and, led by the light of the name of the All-Seeing God, make your escape from the darkness that surroundeth you. Let your vision be world-embracing, rather than confined to your own self. The Evil One is he that hindereth the rise and obstructeth the spiritual progress of the children of men.

It is incumbent upon every man, in this Day, to hold fast unto whatsoever will promote the interests, and exalt the station, of all nations and just governments. Through each and every one of the verses which the Pen of the Most High hath revealed, the doors of love and unity have been unlocked and flung open to the face of men. We have erewhile declared—and Our Word is the truth—: 'Consort with the followers of all religions in a spirit of friendliness and fellowship.' Whatsoever hath led the children of men to shun one another, and hath caused dissensions and divisions amongst them, hath, through the revelation of these words, been nullified and abolished. From the heaven of God's Will, and for the purpose of ennobling the world of being and of elevating the minds and souls of men, hath been sent down that which is the most effective instrument for the education of the whole human race. The highest essence and most perfect expression of whatsoever the peoples of old have either said or written hath, through this most potent Revelation, been sent down from the heaven of the Will of the All-Possessing, the Ever-Abiding God. Of old it hath been revealed: 'Love of one's country is an element of the Faith of God.' The Tongue of Grandeur hath, however, in the day of His manifestation proclaimed: 'It is not his to boast who loveth his country, but it is his who loveth the world.' Through the power released by these exalted words He hath lent a fresh impulse and set a new direction to the birds of men's hearts, and hath obliterated every trace of restriction and limitation from God's holy Book.

This Wronged One hath forbidden the people of God to engage in contention or conflict and hath exhorted them to righteous deeds and praiseworthy character. In this day the hosts that can ensure the victory of the Cause are those of goodly conduct and saintly character. Blessed are they who firmly adhere unto them and woe betide such as turn away therefrom.

O people of God! I admonish you to observe courtesy, for above all else it is the prince of virtues. Well is it with him who is illumined with the light of courtesy and is attired with the vesture of uprightness. Whoso is endued with courtesy hath indeed attained a sublime station. It is hoped that this Wronged One and everyone else may be enabled to acquire it, hold fast unto it, observe it, and fix our gaze upon it. This is a binding command which hath streamed forth from the Pen of the Most Great Name.

This is the day when the gems of constancy that lie hid in the mine of men's inner selves should be made manifest. O people of Justice! Be as brilliant as the light and as splendid as the fire that blazed in the Burning Bush. The brightness of the fire of your love will no doubt fuse and unify the contending peoples and kindreds of the earth, whilst the fierceness of the flame of enmity and hatred cannot but result in strife and ruin. We beseech God that He may shield His creatures from the evil designs of His enemies. He verily hath power over all things.

All praise be to the one true God—exalted be His glory —inasmuch as He hath, through the Pen of the Most High, unlocked the doors of men's hearts. Every verse which this Pen hath revealed is a bright and shining portal that discloseth the glories of a saintly and pious life, of pure and stainless deeds. The summons and the message which We gave were never intended to reach or to benefit one land or one people only. Mankind in its entirety must firmly adhere to whatsoever hath been revealed and vouchsafed unto it. Then and only then will it attain unto true liberty. The whole earth is illuminated with the resplendent glory of God's Revelation. In the year sixty He Who heralded the light of Divine Guidance—may all creation be a sacrifice unto Him—arose to announce a fresh revelation of the Divine Spirit, and was followed, twenty years later, by Him through Whose coming the world was made the recipient of this promised glory, this wondrous favour. Behold how the generality of mankind hath been endued with the capacity to hearken unto God's most exalted Word—the Word upon which must depend the gathering together and spiritual resurrection of all men.

Whilst in the Prison of 'Akká, We revealed in the Crimson Book that which is conducive to the advancement of mankind and to the reconstruction of the world. The utterances set forth therein by the Pen of the Lord of creation include the following which constitute the fundamental principles for the administration of the affairs of men:

First: It is incumbent upon the ministers of the House of Justice to promote the Lesser Peace so that the people of the earth may be relieved from the burden of exorbitant expenditures. This matter is imperative and absolutely essential, inasmuch as hostilities and conflict lie at the root of affliction and calamity.

Second: Languages must be reduced to one common language to be taught in all the schools of the world.

Third: It behoveth man to adhere tenaciously unto that which will promote fellowship, kindliness and unity.

Fourth: Everyone, whether man or woman, should hand over to a trusted person a portion of what he or she earneth through trade, agriculture or other occupation, for the training and education of children, to be spent for this purpose with the knowledge of the Trustees of the House of Justice.

Fifth: Special regard must be paid to agriculture. Although it hath been mentioned in the fifth place, unquestionably it precedeth the others. Agriculture is highly developed in foreign lands, however in Persia it hath so far been grievously neglected. It is hoped that His Majesty the Sháh—may God assist him by His grace—will turn his attention to this vital and important matter.

Were men to strictly observe that which the Pen of the Most High hath revealed in the Crimson Book, they could then well afford to dispense with the regulations which prevail in the world. Certain exhortations have repeatedly streamed forth from the Pen of the Most High that perchance the manifestations of power and the dawning-places of might may, sometime, be enabled to enforce them. Indeed, were sincere seekers to be found, every emanation of God's pervasive and irresistible Will would, for the sake of His love, be revealed. But where are to be found earnest seekers and inquiring minds? Whither are gone the equitable and the fair-minded? At present no day passeth without the fire of a fresh tyranny blazing fiercely, or the sword of a new aggression being unsheathed. Gracious God! The great and the noble in Persia glory in acts of such savagery that one is lost in amazement at the tales thereof.

Day and night this Wronged One yieldeth thanks and praise unto the Lord of men, for it is witnessed that the words of counsel and exhortation We uttered have proved effective and that this people hath evinced such character and conduct as are acceptable in Our sight. This is affirmed by virtue of the event which hath truly cheered the eye of the world, and is none other than the intercession of the friends with the high authorities in favour of their enemies. Indeed one's righteous deeds testify to the truth of one's words. We cherish the hope that men of piety may illumine the world through the radiant light of their conduct, and We entreat the Almighty—glorified and exalted is He—to grant that everyone may in this Day remain steadfast in His love and stand firm in His Cause. He is, in truth, the Protector of those who are wholly devoted to Him and observe His precepts.

O people of God! Countless are the realms which Our Pen of Glory hath revealed and manifold the eyes to which it hath imparted true enlightenment. Yet most of the people in Persia continue to be deprived of the benefits of profitable counsels and remain sorely lacking in useful sciences and arts. Formerly these sublime words were especially revealed by the Pen of Glory in honour of one of the faithful, that perchance those that have gone astray may embrace the Truth and become acquainted with the subtleties of the Law of God.

The unbelievers and the faithless have set their minds on four things: first, the shedding of blood; second, the burning of books; third, the shunning of the followers of other religions; fourth, the extermination of other communities and groups. Now however, through the strengthening grace and potency of the Word of God these four barriers have been demolished, these clear injunctions have been obliterated from the Tablet and brutal dispositions have been transmuted into spiritual attributes. Exalted is His

purpose; glorified is His power; magnified is His dominion!
Now let us beseech God—praised be His glory—to
graciously guide aright the followers of the Shí'ih sect and
to purge them of unseemly conduct. From the lips of the
members of this sect foul imprecations fall unceasingly,
while they invoke the word 'Mal'ún' (accursed)—uttered
with a guttural sound of the letter 'ayn—as their daily
relish.

O God my God! Thou hearest the sighing of Him Who
is Thy Light (Bahá), hearkenest unto His lamentations in
the daytime and in the night season and knowest that He
desireth naught for Himself but rather seeketh to sanctify
the souls of Thy servants and to deliver them from the fire
with which they are beset at all times. O Lord! The hands
of Thy well-favoured servants are raised towards the
heaven of Thy bounty and those of Thy sincere lovers are
lifted up to the sublime heights of Thy generosity. Disappoint them not, I entreat Thee, in that which they seek
from the ocean of Thy favour and from the heaven of Thy
grace and the day-star of Thy bounty. Aid them, O Lord,
to acquire such virtues as will exalt their stations among the
peoples of the world. Verily Thou art the Powerful, the
Mighty, the Most Generous.

O people of God! Give ear unto that which, if heeded,
will ensure the freedom, well-being, tranquillity, exaltation
and advancement of all men. Certain laws and principles
are necessary and indispensable for Persia. However, it is
fitting that these measures should be adopted in conformity
with the considered views of His Majesty—may God aid
him through His grace—and of the learned divines and of
the high-ranking rulers. Subject to their approval a place
should be fixed where they would meet. There they should
hold fast to the cord of consultation and adopt and enforce

that which is conducive to the security, prosperity, wealth and tranquillity of the people. For were any measure other than this to be adopted, it could not but result in chaos and commotion.

According to the fundamental laws which We have formerly revealed in the *Kitáb-i-Aqdas* and other Tablets, all affairs are committed to the care of just kings and presidents and of the Trustees of the House of Justice. Having pondered on that which We have enunciated, every man of equity and discernment will readily perceive, with his inner and outer eyes, the splendours of the daystar of justice which radiate therefrom.

The system of government which the British people have adopted in London appeareth to be good, for it is adorned with the light of both kingship and of the consultation of the people.

In formulating the principles and laws a part hath been devoted to penalties which form an effective instrument for the security and protection of men. However, dread of the penalties maketh people desist only outwardly from committing vile and contemptible deeds, while that which guardeth and restraineth man both outwardly and inwardly hath been and still is the fear of God. It is man's true protector and his spiritual guardian. It behoveth him to cleave tenaciously unto that which will lead to the appearance of this supreme bounty. Well is it with him who giveth ear unto whatsoever My Pen of Glory hath proclaimed and observeth that whereunto he is bidden by the Ordainer, the Ancient of Days.

Incline your hearts, O people of God, unto the counsels of your true, your incomparable Friend. The Word of God may be likened unto a sapling, whose roots have been implanted in the hearts of men. It is incumbent upon you to foster its growth through the living waters of wisdom, of sanctified and holy words, so that its root may become firmly fixed and its branches may spread out as high as the heavens and beyond.

O ye that dwell on earth! The distinguishing feature that marketh the pre-eminent character of this Supreme Revelation consisteth in that We have, on the one hand, blotted out from the pages of God's holy Book whatsoever hath been the cause of strife, of malice and mischief amongst the children of men, and have, on the other, laid down the essential prerequisites of concord, of understanding, of complete and enduring unity. Well is it with them that keep My statutes.

Time and again have We admonished Our beloved ones to avoid, nay to flee from, anything whatsoever from which the odour of mischief can be detected. The world is in great turmoil, and the minds of its people are in a state of utter confusion. We entreat the Almighty that He may graciously illuminate them with the glory of His Justice, and enable them to discover that which will be profitable unto them at all times and under all conditions. He, verily is the All-Possessing, the Most High.

We have ere this uttered these sublime words: Let them that bear allegiance to this Wronged One be even as a raining cloud in moments of charity and benevolence and as a blazing fire in restraining their base and appetitive natures.

Gracious God! A thing hath recently happened which caused great astonishment. It is reported that a certain person[1] went to the seat of the imperial throne in Persia and succeeded in winning the good graces of some of the nobility by his ingratiating behaviour. How pitiful indeed, how deplorable! One wondereth why those who have

---

[1] Jamálu'd-Dín-i-Afghání. (See *God Passes By* pp. 296, 317.)

been the symbols of highest glory should now stoop to boundless shame. What is become of their high resolve? Whither is gone the sense of dignity and honour? The sun of glory and wisdom hath unceasingly been shining above the horizon of Persia, but nowadays it hath sunk to such a low level that certain dignitaries have allowed themselves to be treated as playthings in the hands of the foolish. The aforesaid person hath written such things concerning this people in the Egyptian press and in the Beirut Encyclopedia that the well-informed and the learned were astonished. He proceeded then to Paris where he published a newspaper entitled *'Urvatu'l-Vuthqá* [The Sure Handle] and sent copies thereof to all parts of the world. He also sent a copy to the Prison of 'Akká, and by so doing he meant to show affection and to make amends for his past actions. In short, this Wronged One hath observed silence in regard to him. We entreat God, the True One, to protect him and to shed upon him the light of justice and fairness. It behoveth him to say:

O God my God! Thou seest me standing before the door of Thy forgiveness and benevolence, turning my gaze toward the horizon of Thy bountiful favours and manifold blessings. I beg of Thee by Thy sweet accents and by the shrill voice of Thy Pen, O Lord of all mankind, to graciously aid Thy servants as it befitteth Thy days and beseemeth the glory of Thy manifestation and Thy majesty. Verily potent art Thou to do whatsoever Thou willest. All they that dwell in the heavens and on the earth bear witness to Thy power and Thy might, to Thy glory and Thy bounteousness. Praise be to Thee, O Lord of the worlds and the Well-Beloved of the heart of every man of understanding!

Thou beholdest, O my God, the essence of poverty

seeking the ocean of Thy wealth and the substance of iniquity yearning for the waters of Thy forgiveness and Thy tender mercy. Grant Thou, O my God, that which beseemeth Thy great glory and befitteth the loftiness of Thy boundless grace. Thou art in truth the All-Bountiful, the Lord of grace abounding, the Ordainer, the All-Wise. No God is there but Thee, the Most Powerful, the All-Compelling, the Omnipotent.

O people of God! In this day everyone should fix his eyes upon the horizon of these blessed words: 'Alone and unaided He doeth whatsoever He pleaseth.' Whoso attaineth this station hath verily attained the light of the essential unity of God and is enlightened thereby, while all others are reckoned in the Book of God among the followers of idle fancy and vain imagination. Incline your ears to the Voice of this Wronged One and safeguard the integrity of your stations. It is highly necessary and imperative that everyone should observe this matter.

Unveiled and unconcealed, this Wronged One hath, at all times, proclaimed before the face of all the peoples of the world that which will serve as the key for unlocking the doors of sciences, of arts, of knowledge, of well-being, of prosperity and wealth. Neither have the wrongs inflicted by the oppressors succeeded in silencing the shrill voice of the Most Exalted Pen, nor have the doubts of the perverse or of the seditious been able to hinder Him from revealing the Most Sublime Word. I earnestly beseech God that He may protect and purge the people of Bahá from the idle fancies and corrupt imaginings of the followers of the former Faith.

O people of God! Righteous men of learning who dedicate themselves to the guidance of others and are freed and well guarded from the promptings of a base and covetous nature are, in the sight of Him Who is the Desire of the world, stars of the heaven of true knowledge. It is essential to treat them with deference. They are indeed fountains of soft-flowing water, stars that shine resplendent, fruits of the blessed Tree, exponents of celestial power, and oceans of heavenly wisdom. Happy is he that followeth them. Verily such a soul is numbered in the Book of God, the Lord of the mighty Throne, among those with whom it shall be well.

The glory which proceedeth from God, the Lord of the Throne on High and of the earth below, rest upon you, O people of Bahá, O ye the companions of the Crimson Ark, and upon such as have inclined their ears to your sweet voices and have observed that whereunto they are bidden in this mighty and wondrous Tablet.

8

ISHRÁQÁT
(Splendours)

This is the Epistle of God, the Help in Peril, the Self-Subsisting

He is God, exalted is He, the Lord of wisdom and utterance.

RAISE be unto God, incomparable in majesty, power and beauty, peerless in glory, might and grandeur; too high is He for human imaginations to comprehend Him or for any peer or equal to be ascribed unto Him. He hath clearly set forth His straight Path in words and utterances of highest eloquence. Verily He is the All-Possessing, the Most Exalted. When He purposed to call the new creation into being, He sent forth the Manifest and Luminous Point from the horizon of His Will; it passed through every sign and manifested itself in every form until it reached the zenith, as bidden by God, the Lord of all men.

This Point is the focal centre of the circle of Names and marketh the culmination of the manifestations of Letters in the world of creation. Through it have appeared indications of the impenetrable Mystery, the adorned Symbol, He Who standeth revealed in the Most Great Name—a Name which is recorded in the luminous Tablet and is inscribed in the holy, the blessed, the snow-white Scroll. And when the Point was joined to the second Letter[1] which

---

[1] i.e., the letter 'B', the second letter of the alphabet.

appeareth in the beginning of the Mathání,[1] it traversed the heavens of exposition and utterance. Then the eternal Light of God shed its radiance, flared up in the midmost heart of the firmament of testimony and produced two Luminaries. Glorified be the Merciful One, unto Whom no allusion can be made, Whom no expression can define, nor any assertion reveal, nor any evidence describe. He is in truth the Ordainer, the All-Bountiful, both in the beginning and in the end. And He provided for them protectors and defenders from among the hosts of power and might. Verily, He is the Help in Peril, the Mighty, the Unconstrained.

*The preamble of this Epistle is being revealed twice,
even as was the Mathání[1]*

Praise be unto God Who hath manifested the Point, hath unfolded therefrom the knowledge of all things, whether of the past or of the future—a Point He hath chosen to be the Herald of His Name and the Harbinger of His Great Revelation which hath caused the limbs of all mankind to quake and the splendour of His light to shine forth above the horizon of the world. Verily, this is the Point which God hath ordained to be an ocean of light for the sincere among His servants and a flame of fire to the froward amidst His creatures and the impious among His people—they who bartered away the gift of God for unbelief, and the celestial food for hypocrisy, and led their associates to a wretched abode. These are the people who

---

[1] The opening chapter of the Qur'án, which begins with the letter 'B': Bismi'lláhi'r-Raḥmáni'r-Raḥím (In the Name of God, the Compassionate, the Merciful). This chapter of the Qur'án was revealed twice, once in Mecca and once in Medina.

have manifested sedition throughout the world and have violated His Covenant on the Day when the immortal Being mounted His throne and the Crier raised His Voice from the haven of security and peace in the holy Vale.

O followers of the Bayán! Fear ye the All-Merciful. This is the One Who hath been glorified by Muḥammad, the Apostle of God, and before Him by the Spirit[1] and yet before Him by the One Who discoursed with God.[2] This is the Point of the Bayán calling aloud before the Throne, saying: 'By the righteousness of God, ye have been created to glorify this Most Great Announcement, this Perfect Way which lay hid within the souls of the Prophets, which was treasured in the hearts of the chosen ones of God and was written down by the glorious Pen of your Lord, the Possessor of Names.'

Say: Die in your wrath, O malicious ones! Verily He Whose knowledge nothing escapeth hath appeared. He Who hath caused the countenance of divine knowledge to be wreathed in smiles is come. Through Him the kingdom of utterance is embellished, every receptive soul hath set his face towards the Lord of Revelations, everyone resting on his knees hath stood up, and every indolent one hath rushed forth to attain the Sinai of assurance. This is the Day that God hath ordained to be a blessing unto the righteous, a retribution for the wicked, a bounty for the faithful and a fury of His wrath for the faithless and the froward. Verily He hath been made manifest, invested by God with invincible sovereignty. He hath revealed that wherewith naught on the earth or in the heavens can compare.

Fear ye the All-Merciful, O people of the Bayán, and commit not that which the followers of the Qur'án have

[1] Jesus.
[2] Moses.

committed—they who in the daytime and in the night season professed belief in the Faith of God, yet when the Lord of all men did appear, turned aside from Him and pronounced so cruel a sentence against Him that, on the Day of Return, the Mother Book sorely bewailed His plight. Call ye to mind and ponder upon their deeds and words, their stations and merits and the things they brought to pass when He Who conversed on Sinai unloosed His tongue, when there was a blast on the Trumpet, whereupon all that are in heaven and on earth swooned away except such as are reckoned among the letters of affirmation.

O people of the Bayán! Abandon your idle fancies and vain imaginings, then with the eye of fairness look at the Dayspring of His Revelation and consider the things He hath manifested, the words He hath divinely revealed and the sufferings that have befallen Him at the hands of His enemies. He is the One Who hath willingly accepted every manner of tribulation for the proclamation of His Cause and the exaltation of His Word. At one time He suffered imprisonment in the land of Ṭá (Ṭihrán), at another in the land of Mím (Mázindarán), then once again in the former land, for the sake of the Cause of God, the Maker of the heavens. In His love for the Cause of God, the Almighty, the All-Bountiful, He was subjected there to chains and fetters.

O people of the Bayán! Have ye forgotten My exhortations, which My Pen hath revealed and My tongue hath uttered? Have ye bartered away My certitude in exchange for your idle fancies and My Way for your selfish desires? Have ye cast away the precepts of God and His remembrance and have ye forsaken His laws and ordinances? Fear ye God and abandon vain imaginings to the begetters thereof and leave superstitions to the devisers thereof and misgivings to the breeders thereof. Advance ye then with radiant faces and stainless hearts towards the horizon above which the Day-Star of certitude shineth resplendent at the bidding of God, the Lord of Revelations.

Praise be unto God Who hath made the Most Great Infallibility the shield for the temple of His Cause in the realm of creation, and hath assigned unto no one a share of this lofty and sublime station—a station which is a vesture which the fingers of transcendent power have woven for His august Self. It befitteth no one except Him Who is seated upon the mighty throne of 'He doeth what He pleaseth'. Whoso accepteth and recognizeth that which is written down at this moment by the Pen of Glory is indeed reckoned in the Book of God, the Lord of the beginning and the end, among the exponents of divine unity, they that uphold the concept of the oneness of God.

When the stream of words reached this stage, the sweet savours of true knowledge were shed abroad and the day-star of divine unity shone forth above the horizon of His holy utterance. Blessed is he whom His Call hath attracted to the summit of glory, who hath drawn nigh to the ultimate Purpose, and who hath recognized through the shrill voice of My Pen of Glory that which the Lord of this world and of the next hath willed. Whoso faileth to quaff the choice wine which We have unsealed through the potency of Our Name, the All-Compelling, shall be unable to discern the splendours of the light of divine unity or to grasp the essential purpose underlying the Scriptures of God, the Lord of heaven and earth, the sovereign Ruler of this world and of the world to come. Such a man shall be accounted among the faithless in the Book of God, the All-Knowing, the All-Informed.

O thou honoured enquirer![1] We bear witness that thou didst firmly adhere unto seemly patience during the days when the Pen was held back from movement and the Tongue hesitated to set forth an explanation regarding the wondrous sign, the Most Great Infallibility. Thou hast asked this Wronged One to remove for thee its veils and coverings, to elucidate its mystery and character, its state and position, its excellence, sublimity and exaltation. By the life of God! Were We to unveil the pearls of testimony which lie hid within the shells of the ocean of knowledge and assurance or to let the beauties of divine mystery which are hidden within the chambers of utterance in the Paradise of true understanding, step out of their habitation, then from every direction violent commotion would arise among the leaders of religion and thou wouldst witness the people of God held fast in the teeth of such wolves as have denied God both in the beginning and in the end. Therefore We restrained the Pen for a considerable lapse of time in accordance with divine wisdom and for the sake of protecting the faithful from those who have bartered away heavenly blessings for disbelief and have chosen for their people the abode of perdition.[2]

O thou seeker who art gifted with keen insight. I swear by Him Who attracted the Concourse on High through the potency of His most sublime Word! Verily, the birds abiding within the domains of My Kingdom and the doves dwelling in the rose-garden of My wisdom utter such melodies and warblings as are inscrutable to all but God, the Lord of the kingdoms of earth and heaven; and were these melodies to be revealed even to an extent smaller than

[1] This Tablet was addressed to Jalíl-i-Khu'í, one of the early believers in Ádhirbáyján, Persia. After the Ascension of Bahá'u'lláh he broke the Covenant.

[2] cf. Qur'án 14:33.

a needle's eye, the people of tyranny would utter such calumnies as none among former generations hath ever uttered, and would commit such deeds as no one in past ages and centuries hath ever committed. They have rejected the bounty of God and His proofs and have repudiated the testimony of God and His signs. They have gone astray and have caused the people to go astray, yet perceive it not. They worship vain imaginings but know it not. They have taken idle fancies for their lords and have neglected God, yet understand not. They have abandoned the most great Ocean and are hastening towards the pool, but comprehend not. They follow their own idle fancies while turning aside from God, the Help in Peril, the Self-Subsisting.

Say, by the righteousness of God! The All-Merciful is come invested with power and sovereignty. Through His power the foundations of religions have quaked and the Nightingale of Utterance hath warbled its melody upon the highest branch of true understanding. Verily, He Who was hidden in the knowledge of God and is mentioned in the Holy Scriptures hath appeared. Say, this is the Day when the Speaker on Sinai hath mounted the throne of Revelation and the people have stood before the Lord of the worlds. This is the Day wherein the earth hath told out her tidings and hath laid bare her treasures; when the oceans have brought forth their pearls and the divine Lote-Tree its fruit; when the Sun hath shed its radiance and the Moons have diffused their lights, and the Heavens have revealed their stars, and the Hour its signs, and the Resurrection its dreadful majesty; when the pens have unloosed their outpourings and the spirits have laid bare their mysteries. Blessed is the man who recognizeth Him and attaineth His presence, and woe betide such as deny Him and turn aside from Him. I beseech God to aid His servants to return unto Him. Verily He is the Pardoner, the Forgiving, the Merciful.

O thou who hast set thy face towards the Realm on High and hast quaffed My sealed wine from the hand of bounteousness! Know thou that the term 'Infallibility' hath numerous meanings and divers stations. In one sense it is applicable to the One Whom God hath made immune from error. Similarly it is applied to every soul whom God hath guarded against sin, transgression, rebellion, impiety, disbelief and the like. However, the Most Great Infallibility is confined to the One Whose station is immeasurably exalted beyond ordinances or prohibitions and is sanctified from errors and omissions. Indeed He is a Light which is not followed by darkness and a Truth not overtaken by error. Were He to pronounce water to be wine or heaven to be earth or light to be fire, He speaketh the truth and no doubt would there be about it; and unto no one is given the right to question His authority or to say why or wherefore. Whosoever raiseth objections will be numbered with the froward in the Book of God, the Lord of the worlds. 'Verily He shall not be asked of His doings but all others shall be asked of their doings.'[1] He is come from the invisible heaven, bearing the banner 'He doeth whatsoever He willeth' and is accompanied by hosts of power and authority while it is the duty of all besides Him to strictly observe whatever laws and ordinances have been enjoined upon them, and should anyone deviate therefrom, even to the extent of a hair's breadth, his work would be brought to naught.

Consider thou and call to mind the time when Muḥammad appeared. He said, and His word is the truth:

[1] cf. Qur'án 21:23.

'Pilgrimage to the House[1] is a service due to God.'[2] And likewise are the daily prayer, fasting, and the laws which shone forth above the horizon of the Book of God, the Lord of the World and the true Educator of the peoples and kindreds of the earth. It is incumbent upon everyone to obey Him in whatsoever God hath ordained; and whosoever denieth Him hath disbelieved in God, in His verses, in His Messengers and in His Books. Were He to pronounce right to be wrong or denial to be belief, He speaketh the truth as bidden by God. This is a station wherein sins or trespasses neither exist nor are mentioned. Consider thou the blessed, the divinely-revealed verse in which pilgrimage to the House is enjoined upon everyone. It devolved upon those invested with authority after Him[3] to observe whatever had been prescribed unto them in the Book. Unto no one is given the right to deviate from the laws and ordinances of God. Whoso deviateth therefrom is reckoned with the trespassers in the Book of God, the Lord of the Mighty Throne.

O thou who hast fixed thy gaze upon the Dawning-Place of the Cause of God! Know thou for a certainty that the Will of God is not limited by the standards of the people, and God doth not tread in their ways. Rather is it incumbent upon everyone to firmly adhere to God's straight Path. Were He to pronounce the right to be the left or the south to be the north, He speaketh the truth and there is no doubt of it. Verily He is to be praised in His acts and to be obeyed in His behests. He hath no associate in His judgement nor any helper in His sovereignty. He doeth whatsoever He willeth and ordaineth whatsoever He

1 Mecca.
2 Qur'án 3:91.
3 Muḥammad.

pleaseth. Know thou moreover that all else besides Him have been created through the potency of a word from His presence, while of themselves they have no motion nor stillness, except at His bidding and by His leave.

O thou who soarest in the atmosphere of love and fellowship and hast fixed thy gaze upon the light of the countenance of thy Lord, the King of creation! Render thanks unto God, inasmuch as He hath unravelled for thee that which was hidden and enshrined in His knowledge so that everyone may become aware that within His realm of supreme infallibility He hath not taken a partner nor a counsellor unto Himself. He is in truth the Dayspring of divine precepts and commandments and the Fountainhead of knowledge and wisdom, while all else besides Him are but His subjects and under His rule, and He is the supreme Ruler, the Ordainer, the All-Knowing, the All-Informed.

As to thyself, whenever thou art enraptured by the vitalizing breaths of the revealed verses and art carried away by the pure, life-giving water proffered by the hand of the bounty of thy Lord, the sovereign Ruler of the Day of Resurrection, lift up thy voice and say:

O my God! O my God! I yield Thee thanks that Thou hast directed me towards Thyself, hast guided me unto Thy horizon, hast clearly set forth for me Thy Path, hast revealed to me Thy testimony and enabled me to set my face towards Thee, while most of the doctors and divines among Thy servants together with such as follow them have, without the least proof or evidence from Thee, turned away from Thee. Blessing be unto Thee, O Lord of Names, and glory be unto Thee, O Creator of the heavens, inasmuch as Thou hast, through the power of Thy Name, the Self-Subsisting, given me to drink of Thy sealed wine, hast caused me to draw nigh unto Thee and hast enabled me to recognize the Dayspring of Thine utterance, the Manifestation of Thy signs, the Fountainhead of Thy laws and commandments and the Source of Thy wisdom and bestowals. Blessed is the land that hath been ennobled by Thy footsteps, wherein the throne of Thy sovereignty is established and the fragrance of Thy raiment is diffused. By Thy glory and majesty, by Thy might and power, I desire not my sight save to behold Thy beauty, nor my hearing save to hearken to Thy call and Thy verses.

O my God! O my God! Debar not the eyes from that for which Thou hast created them, nor the faces from turning to Thy horizon, or from paying homage at the portals of Thy majesty, or from appearing in the presence of Thy throne, or from bowing down before the splendours of the Day-Star of Thy bounty.

I am the one, O Lord, whose heart and soul, whose limbs, whose inner and outer tongue testify to Thy unity and Thy oneness, and bear witness that Thou art God and that there is no God but Thee. Thou didst bring mankind into being to know Thee and to serve Thy Cause, that their station might thereby be elevated upon Thine earth and their souls be uplifted by virtue of the things Thou hast revealed in Thy Scriptures, Thy Books and Thy Tablets. Yet no sooner didst Thou manifest Thyself and reveal Thy signs than they turned away from Thee and repudiated Thee and rejected that which Thou didst unveil before their eyes through the potency of Thy might and Thy power. They rose up to inflict harm upon Thee, to extinguish Thy light and to put out the flame that blazeth in Thy Burning Bush. Their iniquity waxed so grievous that they conspired to shed Thy blood and to violate Thy honour. And likewise acted he[1] whom Thou hadst

[1] Mírzá Yaḥyá.

nurtured with the hand of Thy loving-kindness, hadst protected from the mischief of the rebellious among Thy creatures and the froward amidst Thy servants, and whom Thou hadst set the task of writing Thy holy verses before Thy throne.

Alas! Alas! for the things he perpetrated in Thy days to such an extent that he violated Thy Covenant and Thy Testament, rejected Thy holy Writ, rose up in rebellion and committed that which caused the denizens of Thy Kingdom to lament. Then no sooner had he found his hopes shattered and had perceived the odour of utter failure than he raised his voice and gave tongue to that which caused Thy chosen ones, who are nigh unto Thee, and the inmates of the pavilion of glory, to be lost in bewilderment.

Thou seest me, O my God, writhing in anguish upon the dust, like unto a fish. Deliver me, have mercy upon me, O Thou Whose aid is invoked by all men, O Thou within Whose grasp lie the reins of power over all men and women. Whenever I ponder my grievous shortcomings and my great trespasses, despair assaileth me from every direction, and whenever I pause to meditate upon the ocean of Thy bounteousness and the heaven of Thy grace and the day-star of Thy tender compassion, I inhale the fragrance of hope diffused from right and left, from north and south, as if every created thing imparteth unto me the joyous tidings that the clouds of the heaven of Thy mercy will pour down their rain upon me. By Thy might, O Thou Who art the Mainstay of the sincere ones and the Desire of them that enjoy near access unto Thee! Thy manifold favours and blessings and the revelations of Thy grace and loving-kindness have truly emboldened me. How, other-wise, can utter nothingness magnify the Name of Him

Who hath, by a word, brought creation into being, and how can an evanescent creature extol Him Who hath demonstrated that no description can ever express Him and no word of praise magnify His glory? He hath from everlasting been immeasurably exalted above the understanding of His creatures and sanctified from the conceptions of His servants.

O Lord! Thou beholdest this lifeless one before Thy face; suffer him, through Thy generosity and bountiful favour, not to be deprived of the chalice of immortal life. And Thou seest this afflicted one standing before Thy throne; turn him not away from the ocean of Thy healing. I entreat Thee to enable me at all times and under all conditions to remember Thee, to magnify Thy Name and to serve Thy Cause, though I am well aware that whatever proceedeth from a servant cannot transcend the limitations of his soul, nor beseem Thy Lordship, nor be worthy of the court of Thy glory and Thy majesty.

Thy might beareth me witness! Were it not to celebrate Thy praise, my tongue would be of no use to me, and were it not for the sake of rendering service to Thee, my existence would avail me not. But for the pleasure of beholding the splendours of Thy realm of glory, why should I cherish sight? And but for the joy of giving ear to Thy most sweet voice, of what use is hearing?

Alas! Alas! I know not, O my God, my Mainstay, my heart's Desire, whether Thou hast ordained for me that which shall bring solace to mine eyes, gladden my bosom and rejoice my heart, or whether Thine irrevocable decree, O King of eternity and the sovereign Lord of all nations, will debar me from presenting myself before Thy throne. I swear by Thy glory and majesty and by Thy dominion and power, the darkness of my remoteness from Thee hath destroyed me. What hath become of the light of Thy nearness, O Desire of every understanding heart? The tormenting agony of separation from Thee hath consumed me. Where is the effulgent light of Thy reunion, O Well-Beloved of such as are wholly devoted to Thee?

Thou seest, O my God, what hath befallen me in Thy Path at the hand of those who have denied Thy Truth, have violated Thy Covenant, cavilled at Thy signs, rejected the blessings Thou didst vouchsafe, disbelieved the verses Thou didst send down and have refused to acknowledge the testimony Thou didst fulfil.

O Lord! The tongue of my tongue and the heart of my heart and the spirit of my spirit and my outward and inmost beings bear witness to Thy unity and Thy oneness, Thy power and Thine omnipotence, Thy grandeur and Thy sovereignty, and attest Thy glory, loftiness and authority. I testify that Thou art God and that there is none other God besides Thee. From everlasting Thou hast been a treasure hidden from the sight and minds of men and shalt continue to remain the same for ever and ever. The powers of earth can never frustrate Thee, nor can the might of the nations alarm Thee. Thou art the One Who hath unlocked the door of knowledge before the faces of Thy servants that they may recognize Him Who is the Day-Star of Thy Revelation, the Dawning-Place of Thy signs, the Heaven of Thy manifestation and the Sun of Thy divine beauty. In Thy holy Books, in Thy Scriptures and Thy Scrolls Thou hast promised all the peoples of the world that Thou Thyself shalt appear and shalt remove the veils of glory from Thy face, even as Thou didst announce in Thy words unto Thy Friend[1] through Whom the Day-Star of Revelation shone brightly above the horizon of

[1] Muḥammad.

Ḥijáz, and the dawning light of divine Truth shed its radiance among all men, proclaiming: 'The Day when mankind shall stand before the Lord of the worlds.'[1] And before Muḥammad Thou didst impart this glad-tiding unto Him Who conversed with Thee,[2] saying: 'Bring forth thy people from the darkness into the light and remind them of the days of God.'[3] Moreover Thou didst proclaim this truth unto the Spirit[4] and unto Thy Prophets and Thy Messengers, whether of the remote or more recent past. If all that which Thou hast sent down in glorification of this Most Great Remembrance, this Great Announcement, were to stream forth from the wellspring of Thy most august Pen, the inmates of the cities of knowledge and understanding would be dumbfounded, except such as Thou wouldst deliver through the potency of Thy might and wouldst protect as a token of Thy bountiful favour and Thy grace. I bear witness that Thou hast in truth fulfilled Thy pledge and hast made manifest the One Whose advent was foretold by Thy Prophets, Thy chosen ones and by them that serve Thee. He hath come from the heaven of glory and power, bearing the banners of Thy signs and the standards of Thy testimonies. Through the potency of Thine indomitable power and strength, He stood up before the faces of all men and summoned all mankind to the summit of transcendent glory and unto the all-highest Horizon, in such wise that neither the oppression of the ecclesiastics nor the onslaught of the rulers was able to deter Him. He arose with inflexible resolve and, unloosing His tongue, proclaimed in ringing tones: 'He Who is the

[1] Qur'án 83:6.
[2] Moses.
[3] Qur'án 14:5.
[4] Jesus.

All-Bountiful is come, riding aloft on the clouds. Advance, O people of the earth, with shining faces and radiant hearts!'

Great indeed is the blessedness of him who attaineth Thy presence, drinketh the wine of reunion proffered by the hand of Thy bounteousness, inhaleth the fragrance of Thy signs, unlooseth his tongue in celebrating Thy praise, soareth high in Thy heavens, is carried away by the sweetness of Thy Voice, gaineth admittance into the most exalted Paradise and attaineth the station of revelation and vision before the throne of Thy majesty.

I beg of Thee by the Most Great Infallibility which Thou hast chosen to be the dayspring of Thy Revelation, and by Thy most sublime Word through whose potency Thou didst call the creation into being and didst reveal Thy Cause, and by this Name which hath caused all other names to groan aloud and the limbs of the sages to quake, I beg of Thee to make me detached from all else save Thee, in such wise that I may move not but in conformity with the good-pleasure of Thy Will, and speak not except at the bidding of Thy Purpose, and hear naught save the words of Thy praise and Thy glorification.

I magnify Thy Name, O my God, and offer thanksgiving unto Thee, O my Desire, inasmuch as Thou hast enabled me to clearly perceive Thy straight Path, hast unveiled Thy Great Announcement before mine eyes and hast aided me to set my face towards the Dayspring of Thy Revelation and the Fountainhead of Thy Cause, whilst Thy servants and Thy people turned away from Thee. I entreat Thee, O Lord of the Kingdom of eternity, by the shrill voice of the Pen of Glory, and by the Burning Fire which calleth aloud from the verdant Tree, and by the Ark which Thou hast specially chosen for the people of Bahá, to grant that I may remain steadfast in my love for Thee, be well pleased with whatsoever Thou hast prescribed for me in Thy Book and may stand firm in Thy service and in the service of Thy loved ones. Graciously assist then Thy servants, O my God, to do that which will serve to exalt Thy Cause and will enable them to observe whatsoever Thou hast revealed in Thy Book.

Verily Thou art the Lord of Strength, Thou art potent to ordain whatsoever Thou willest and within Thy grasp Thou holdest the reins of all created things. No God is there but Thee, the All-Powerful, the All-Knowing, the All-Wise.

O Jalíl! We have unveiled to thine eyes the sea and the waves thereof, the sun and the radiance thereof, the heavens and the stars thereof, the shells and the pearls thereof. Render thou thanks unto God for so great a bounty, so gracious a favour that hath pervaded the whole world.

O thou who hast set thy face towards the splendours of My Countenance! Vague fancies have encompassed the dwellers of the earth and debarred them from turning towards the Horizon of Certitude, and its brightness, and its manifestations and its lights. Vain imaginings have withheld them from Him Who is the Self-Subsisting. They speak as prompted by their own caprices, and understand not. Among them are those who have said: 'Have the verses been sent down?' Say 'Yea, by Him Who is the Lord of the heavens!' 'Hath the Hour come?' 'Nay, more; it hath passed, by Him Who is the Revealer of clear tokens! Verily, the Inevitable is come, and He, the True One, hath appeared with proof and testimony. The Plain is disclosed, and mankind is sore vexed and fearful. Earthquakes have broken loose, and the tribes have lamented,

for fear of God, the Lord of Strength, the All-Compelling.'
Say: 'The stunning trumpet-blast hath been loudly raised,
and the Day is God's, the One, the Unconstrained.' And
they say: 'Hath the Catastrophe come to pass?' Say: 'Yea,
by the Lord of Lords!' 'Is the Resurrection come?' 'Nay,
more; He Who is the Self-Subsisting hath appeared with
the Kingdom of His signs.' 'Seest thou men laid low?' 'Yea,
by my Lord, the Most High, the Most Glorious!' 'Have
the tree-stumps been uprooted?' 'Yea, more; the mountains have been scattered in dust; by Him the Lord of
attributes!' They say: 'Where is Paradise, and where is
Hell?' Say: 'The one is reunion with Me; the other thine
own self, O thou who dost associate a partner with God
and doubtest.' They say: 'We see not the Balance.' Say:
'Surely, by my Lord, the God of Mercy! None can see it
except such as are endued with insight.' They say: 'Have
the stars fallen?' Say: 'Yea, when He Who is the Self-
Subsisting dwelt in the Land of Mystery.[1] Take heed, ye
who are endued with discernment!' All the signs appeared
when We drew forth the Hand of Power from the bosom
of majesty and might. Verily, the Crier hath cried out,
when the promised time came, and they that have recognized the splendours of Sinai have swooned away in the
wilderness of hesitation, before the awful majesty of thy
Lord, the Lord of creation. The trumpet asketh: 'Hath the
Bugle been sounded?' Say: 'Yea, by the King of Revelation! when He mounted the throne of His Name, the All-
Merciful.' Darkness hath been chased away by the dawning
light of the mercy of thy Lord, the Source of all light. The
breeze of the All-Merciful hath wafted, and the souls have
been quickened in the tombs of their bodies. Thus hath the
decree been fulfilled by God, the Mighty, the Beneficent.

[1] Adrianople.

They who reject the truth have said: 'When were the heavens cleft asunder?' Say: 'While ye lay in the graves of waywardness and error.' Among the faithless is he who rubbeth his eyes, and looketh to the right and to the left. Say: 'Blinded art thou. No refuge hast thou to flee to.' And among them is he who saith: 'Have men been gathered together?' Say: 'Yea, by My Lord! whilst thou didst lie in the cradle of idle fancies.' And among them is he who saith: 'Hath the Book been sent down through the power of the true Faith?' Say: 'The true Faith itself is astounded. Fear ye, O ye men of understanding heart!' And among them is he who saith: 'Have I been assembled with others, blind?' Say: 'Yea, by Him that rideth upon the clouds!' Paradise is decked with mystic roses, and hell hath been made to blaze with the fire of the impious. Say: 'The light hath shone forth from the horizon of Revelation, and the whole earth hath been illumined at the coming of Him Who is the Lord of the Day of the Covenant!' The doubters have perished, whilst he that turned, guided by the light of assurance, unto the Dayspring of Certitude hath prospered. Blessed art thou, who hast fixed thy gaze upon Me, for this Tablet which hath been sent down for thee—a Tablet which causeth the souls of men to soar. Commit it to memory, and recite it. By My life! It is a door to the mercy of thy Lord. Well is it with him that reciteth it at eventide and at dawn. We, verily, heard thy praise of this Cause, through which the mountain of knowledge was crushed, and men's feet have slipped. My glory be upon thee and upon whomsoever hath turned unto the Almighty, the All-Bounteous. The Tablet is ended, but the theme is unexhausted. Be patient, for thy Lord is patient.

These are verses We sent down previously, and We have sent them unto thee, that thou mayest be acquainted with what their lying tongues have spoken, when God came unto them with might and sovereignty. The foundations of idle fancies have trembled, and the heaven of vain imaginings hath been cleft asunder, and yet the people are in doubt and in contention with Him. They have denied the testimony of God and His proof, after He came from the heaven of power with the kingdom of His signs. They have cast away what had been prescribed, and perpetrated what had been forbidden them in the Book. They have abandoned their God, and clung unto their desires. They truly have strayed and are in error. They read the verses and deny them. They behold the clear tokens and turn aside. They truly are lost in strange doubt.

We have admonished Our loved ones to fear God, a fear which is the fountainhead of all goodly deeds and virtues. It is the commander of the hosts of justice in the city of Bahá. Happy the man that hath entered the shadow of its luminous standard, and laid fast hold thereon. He, verily, is of the Companions of the Crimson Ark, which hath been mentioned in the Qayyúm-i-Asmá.

Say: O people of God! Adorn your temples with the adornment of trustworthiness and piety. Help, then, your Lord with the hosts of goodly deeds and a praiseworthy character. We have forbidden you dissension and conflict in My Books, and My Scriptures, and My Scrolls, and My Tablets, and have wished thereby naught else save your exaltation and advancement. Unto this testify the heavens and the stars thereof, and the sun and the radiance thereof, and the trees and the leaves thereof, and the seas and the waves thereof, and the earth and the treasures thereof. We pray God to assist His loved ones, and aid them in that which beseemeth them in this blest, this mighty, and wondrous station. Moreover We beseech Him to graciously enable those who surround Me to observe that which My Pen of Glory hath enjoined upon them.

O Jalíl! Upon thee be My glory and My loving providence. Verily We have enjoined the people to do what is meet and seemly and yet they have committed such things as have caused My heart and My Pen to lament. Incline thine ear to that which is sent down from the heaven of My Will and the realm of My good-pleasure. I sorrow not for My captivity, nor for the things that have befallen Me at the hand of Mine enemies. Nay, My sorrows are occasioned by those who claim to be related to Me and yet commit that which causeth the voice of My lamentations to be lifted up and My tears to flow. We have exhorted them at length in various Tablets and beseech God to graciously assist them, to enable them to draw nigh unto Him and to confirm them in that which would bring peace to the hearts and tranquillity to the souls and would stay their hands from whatsoever ill-beseemeth His days.

Say, O My loved ones in My lands! Give ye ear unto the counsels of Him Who admonisheth you for the sake of God. He hath in truth created you, hath revealed before your eyes that which exalteth you and promoteth your interests. He hath made known unto you His straight Path and hath acquainted you with His Great Announcement.

O Jalíl! Admonish men to fear God. By God! This fear is the chief commander of the army of thy Lord. Its hosts are a praiseworthy character and goodly deeds. Through it have the cities of men's hearts been opened throughout the ages and centuries, and the standards of ascendancy and triumph raised above all other standards.

We will now mention unto thee Trustworthiness and the station thereof in the estimation of God, thy Lord, the

Lord of the Mighty Throne. One day of days We repaired unto Our Green Island. Upon Our arrival, We beheld its streams flowing, and its trees luxuriant, and the sunlight playing in their midst. Turning Our face to the right, We beheld what the pen is powerless to describe; nor can it set forth that which the eye of the Lord of Mankind witnessed in that most sanctified, that most sublime, that blest, and most exalted Spot. Turning, then, to the left We gazed on one of the Beauties of the Most Sublime Paradise, standing on a pillar of light, and calling aloud saying: 'O inmates of earth and heaven! Behold ye My beauty, and My radiance, and My revelation, and My effulgence. By God, the True One! I am Trustworthiness and the revelation thereof, and the beauty thereof. I will recompense whosoever will cleave unto Me, and recognize My rank and station, and hold fast unto My hem. I am the most great ornament of the people of Bahá, and the vesture of glory unto all who are in the kingdom of creation. I am the supreme instrument for the prosperity of the world, and the horizon of assurance unto all beings.' Thus have We sent down for thee that which will draw men nigh unto the Lord of creation.

The Pen of the Most High turneth from the eloquent language[1] to the luminous one[2] that thou, O Jalíl, mayest appreciate the tender mercy of thy Lord, the Incomparable One and mayest be of them that are truly grateful.

O thou who hast fixed thy gaze upon the all-glorious Horizon! The Call is raised but hearing ears are numbered, nay non-existent. This Wronged One findeth himself in the maw of the serpent, yet He faileth not to make mention of the loved ones of God. So grievous have been Our sufferings in these days that the Concourse on High are

[1] Arabic.
[2] Persian.

moved to tears and to lamentation. Neither the adversities of the world nor the harm inflicted by its nations could deter Him Who is the King of Eternity from voicing His summons or frustrate His purpose. When those who had for years been hiding behind the veils perceived that the horizon of the Cause was resplendent and that the Word of God was all-pervasive, they rushed forth and with swords of malice inflicted such harm as no pen can portray nor any tongue describe.

They that judge with fairness testify that since the early days of the Cause this Wronged One hath arisen, unveiled and resplendent, before the faces of kings and commoners, before the rulers and the divines, and hath, in ringing tones, summoned all men unto the straight Path. He hath had no helper save His Pen, nor any succourer other than Himself.

Those who are ignorant or heedless of the motivating purpose of the Cause of God have rebelled against Him. Such men are the foreboders of evil, whom God hath mentioned in His Book and Tablets and against whose influence, clamour and deception He hath warned His people. Well is it with those who, in the face of the remembrance of the Lord of Eternity, regard the peoples of the world as utter nothingness, as a thing forgotten, and hold fast to the firm handle of God in such wise that neither doubts nor insinuations, nor swords, nor cannon could hold them back or deprive them of His presence. Blessed are the steadfast; blessed are they that stand firm in His Faith.

In response to thy request the Pen of Glory hath graciously described the stations and grades of the Most Great Infallibility. The purpose is that all should know of a certainty that the Seal of the Prophets[1]—may the souls of

[1] Muḥammad.

all else but Him be offered up for His sake—is without like-ness, peer or partner in His Own station. The Holy Ones[1] —may the blessings of God be upon them—were created through the potency of His Word, and after Him they were the most learned and the most distinguished among the people and abide in the utmost station of servitude. The divine Essence, sanctified from every comparison and like-ness, is established in the Prophet, and God's inmost Real-ity, exalted above any peer or partner, is manifest in Him. This is the station of true unity and veritable singleness. The followers of the previous Dispensation grievously failed to acquire an adequate understanding of this station. The Pri-mal Point[2]—may the life of all else but Him be offered up for His sake—saith: 'If the Seal of the Prophets had not uttered the word "Successorship", such a station would not have been created.'

The people aforetime joined partners with God, though they professed belief in His unity; and although they were the most ignorant amongst men, they considered them-selves the most accomplished. But, as a token of divine retribution upon those heedless ones, their erroneous beliefs and pursuits have, in this Day of Judgement, been made clear and evident to every man of discernment and understanding.

Beseech thou God, the True One, that He may gra-ciously shield the followers of this Revelation from the idle fancies and corrupt imaginings of such as belong to the former Faith, and may not deprive them of the effulgent splendours of the day-star of true unity.

O Jalíl! He Whom the world hath wronged now pro-claimeth: The light of Justice is dimmed, and the sun of

[1] The Imáms.
[2] The Báb.

Equity veiled from sight. The robber occupieth the seat of the protector and guard, and the position of the faithful is seized by the traitor. A year ago an oppressor ruled over this city, and at every instant caused fresh harm. By the righteousness of the Lord! He wrought that which cast terror into the hearts of men. But to the Pen of Glory the tyranny of the world hath never been nor will it ever be a hindrance. In the abundance of Our grace and loving-kindness We have revealed specially for the rulers and ministers of the world that which is conducive to safety and protection, tranquillity and peace; haply the children of men may rest secure from the evils of oppression. He, verily, is the Protector, the Helper, the Giver of victory. It is incumbent upon the men of God's House of Justice to fix their gaze by day and by night upon that which hath shone forth from the Pen of Glory for the training of peoples, the upbuilding of nations, the protection of man and the safeguarding of his honour.

The first Ishráq

When the Day-Star of Wisdom rose above the horizon of God's Holy Dispensation it voiced this all-glorious utterance: They that are possessed of wealth and invested with authority and power must show the profoundest regard for religion. In truth, religion is a radiant light and an impregnable stronghold for the protection and welfare of the peoples of the world, for the fear of God impelleth man to hold fast to that which is good, and shun all evil. Should the lamp of religion be obscured, chaos and confusion will ensue, and the lights of fairness and justice, of tranquillity and peace cease to shine. Unto this will bear witness every man of true understanding.

The second Ishráq

We have enjoined upon all mankind to establish the Most Great Peace—the surest of all means for the protection of humanity. The sovereigns of the world should, with one accord, hold fast thereunto, for this is the supreme instrument that can ensure the security and welfare of all peoples and nations. They, verily, are the manifestations of the power of God and the dayspring of His authority. We beseech the Almighty that He may graciously assist them in that which is conducive to the well-being of their subjects. A full explanation regarding this matter hath been previously set forth by the Pen of Glory; well is it with them that act accordingly.

The third Ishráq

It is incumbent upon everyone to observe God's holy commandments, inasmuch as they are the wellspring of life unto the world. The heaven of divine wisdom is illumined with the two luminaries of consultation and compassion and the canopy of world order is upraised upon the two pillars of reward and punishment.

The fourth Ishráq

In this Revelation the hosts that can render it victorious are the hosts of praiseworthy deeds and upright character. The leader and commander of these hosts hath ever been the fear of God, a fear that encompasseth all things and reigneth over all things.

The fifth Ishráq

Governments should fully acquaint themselves with the conditions of those they govern, and confer upon them positions according to desert and merit. It is enjoined upon every ruler and sovereign to consider this matter with the utmost care that the traitor may not usurp the position of the faithful, nor the despoiler rule in the place of the trust-worthy. Among the officials who in the past have governed in this Most Great Prison some, praise be to God, were adorned with justice, but as to others, We take refuge with God. We beseech the One true God to guide them one and all, that haply they may not be deprived of the fruit of faith and trustworthiness, nor be withheld from the light of equity and justice.

The sixth Ishráq

is union and concord amongst the children of men. From the beginning of time the light of unity hath shed its divine radiance upon the world, and the greatest means for the promotion of that unity is for the peoples of the world to understand one another's writing and speech. In former Epistles We have enjoined upon the Trustees of the House of Justice either to choose one language from among those now existing or to adopt a new one, and in like manner to select a common script, both of which should be taught in all the schools of the world. Thus will the earth be regarded as one country and one home. The most glorious fruit of the tree of knowledge is this exalted word: Of one tree are all ye the fruit, and of one bough the leaves. Let not man glory in this that he loveth his country, let him rather glory in this that he loveth his kind. Concerning this We have previously revealed that which is the means of the reconstruction of the world and the unity of nations. Blessed are they that attain thereunto. Blessed are they that act accordingly.

The seventh Ishráq

The Pen of Glory counselleth everyone regarding the instruction and education of children. Behold that which the Will of God hath revealed upon Our arrival in the Prison City and recorded in the Most Holy Book.[1] Unto every father hath been enjoined the instruction of his son and daughter in the art of reading and writing and in all that hath been laid down in the Holy Tablet. He that putteth away that which is commanded unto him, the Trustees are then to take from him that which is required for their instruction, if he be wealthy, and if not the matter devolveth upon the House of Justice. Verily, have We made it a shelter for the poor and needy. He that bringeth up his son or the son of another, it is as though he hath brought up a son of Mine; upon him rest My Glory, My Loving-Kindness, My Mercy, that have compassed the world.

The eighth Ishráq

This passage, now written by the Pen of Glory, is accounted as part of the Most Holy Book: The men of God's House of Justice have been charged with the affairs of the people. They, in truth, are the Trustees of God among His servants and the dayprings of authority in His countries.

O people of God! That which traineth the world is

[1] *Kitáb-i-Aqdas.*

Justice, for it is upheld by two pillars, reward and punishment. These two pillars are the sources of life to the world. Inasmuch as for each day there is a new problem and for every problem an expedient solution, such affairs should be referred to the House of Justice that the members thereof may act according to the needs and requirements of the time. They that, for the sake of God, arise to serve His Cause, are the recipients of divine inspiration from the unseen Kingdom. It is incumbent upon all to be obedient unto them. All matters of State should be referred to the House of Justice, but acts of worship must be observed according to that which God hath revealed in His Book.

O people of Bahá! Ye are the dawning-places of the love of God and the daysprings of His loving-kindness. Defile not your tongues with the cursing and reviling of any soul, and guard your eyes against that which is not seemly. Set forth that which ye possess. If it be favourably received, your end is attained; if not, to protest is vain. Leave that soul to himself and turn unto the Lord, the Protector, the Self-Subsisting. Be not the cause of grief, much less of discord and strife. The hope is cherished that ye may obtain true education in the shelter of the tree of His tender mercies and act in accordance with that which God desireth. Ye are all the leaves of one tree and the drops of one ocean.

The ninth Ishráq

The purpose of religion as revealed from the heaven of God's holy Will is to establish unity and concord amongst the peoples of the world; make it not the cause of dissension and strife. The religion of God and His divine law are the most potent instruments and the surest of all means for the dawning of the light of unity amongst men. The progress of the world, the development of nations, the tranquillity of peoples, and the peace of all who dwell on earth are among the principles and ordinances of God. Religion bestoweth upon man the most precious of all gifts, offereth the cup of prosperity, imparteth eternal life, and showereth imperishable benefits upon mankind. It behoveth the chiefs and rulers of the world, and in particular the Trustees of God's House of Justice, to endeavour to the utmost of their power to safeguard its position, promote its interests and exalt its station in the eyes of the world. In like manner it is incumbent upon them to enquire into the conditions of their subjects and to acquaint themselves with the affairs and activities of the divers communities in their dominions. We call upon the manifestations of the power of God—the sovereigns and rulers on earth—to bestir themselves and do all in their power that haply they may banish discord from this world and illumine it with the light of concord.

It is incumbent upon everyone to firmly adhere to and observe that which hath streamed forth from Our Most Exalted Pen. God, the True One, beareth Me witness, and every atom in existence is moved to testify that such means as lead to the elevation, the advancement, the education, the protection and the regeneration of the peoples of the earth have been clearly set forth by Us and are revealed in the Holy Books and Tablets by the Pen of Glory.

We entreat God to graciously aid His servants. What this Wronged One doth expect from everyone is justice and fairness. Let no one be content with mere hearing; rather doth it behove everyone to ponder that which this Wronged One hath revealed. I swear by the Day-Star of utterance, shining above the horizon of the Kingdom of the All-

Merciful, had there been any expounder or speaker discernible, We would not have made Ourself the object of the censure, ridicule and slander of the people.

Upon Our arrival in 'Iráq We found the Cause of God sunk in deep apathy and the breeze of divine revelation stilled. Most of the believers were faint and dispirited, nay utterly lost and dead. Hence there was a second blast on the Trumpet, whereupon the Tongue of Grandeur uttered these blessed words: 'We have sounded the Trumpet for the second time.' Thus the whole world was quickened through the vitalizing breaths of divine revelation and inspiration.

Certain souls have now sallied forth from behind the veils, intent on inflicting harm upon this Wronged One. They have hindered and denied the outpouring of this priceless bounty.

O ye that judge with fairness! If this Cause is to be denied then what other cause in this world can be vindicated or deemed worthy of acceptance?

Such as have turned away from the Cause of God are diligently seeking to collect the Holy Writings of this Revelation; and they have already, through gestures of friendship, managed to secure certain of these Writings from those who held them in their possession. Moreover, when they meet the followers of any religion, they hold themselves out as believers therein. Say, die ye in your wrath! Verily He hath appeared with so great an authority that no man of vision, of hearing, of insight, of justice or of equity can ever deny Him. Unto this beareth witness in this resplendent Hour the Pen of Him Who is the Ancient of Days.

O Jalíl! Upon thee be My glory. We exhort the loved ones of God to perform good deeds that perchance they may be graciously assisted and may hold fast to that which hath been sent down from the heaven of His Revelation. The benefits arising from this divine utterance shall fall upon such as observe His precepts. We beseech God to enable them to do that which is pleasing and acceptable unto Him, to grant that they may deal equitably and may observe justice in this all-compelling Cause, to acquaint them with His Holy Writings and to direct their steps towards His straight Path.

Our Exalted Herald—may the life of all else besides Him be offered up for His sake—hath revealed certain laws. However, in the realm of His Revelation these laws were made subject to Our sanction, hence this Wronged One hath put some of them into effect by embodying them in the *Kitáb-i-Aqdas* in different words. Others We set aside. He holdeth in His hand the authority. He doeth what He willeth and He ordaineth whatsoever He pleaseth. He is the Almighty, the All-Praised. There are also ordinances newly revealed. Blessed are they that attain. Blessed are they that observe His precepts.

The people of God should make the utmost endeavour that perchance the fire of hatred and malice which smouldereth in the breasts of kindreds and peoples may, through the living waters of utterance and the exhortations of Him Who is the Desire of the world, be quenched and the trees of human existence may be adorned with wondrous and excellent fruit. He is, in truth, the Admonisher, the Compassionate, the All-Bountiful.

May the brightness of His glory shining above the horizon of bounty rest upon you, O people of Bahá, upon every one who standeth firm and steadfast and upon those that are well grounded in the Faith and are endued with true understanding.

As to thy question concerning interest and profit on gold

and silver: Some years ago the following passage was revealed from the heaven of the All-Merciful in honour of the one who beareth the name of God, entitled Zaynu'l-Muqarrabín[1]—upon him be the glory of the Most Glorious. He—exalted be His Word—saith: Many people stand in need of this. Because if there were no prospect for gaining interest, the affairs of men would suffer collapse or dislocation. One can seldom find a person who would manifest such consideration towards his fellow-man, his countryman or towards his own brother and would show such tender solicitude for him as to be well-disposed to grant him a loan on benevolent terms.[2] Therefore as a token of favour towards men We have prescribed that interest on money should be treated like other business transactions that are current amongst men. Thus, now that this lucid commandment hath descended from the heaven of the Will of God, it is lawful and proper to charge interest on money, that the people of the world may, in a spirit of amity and fellowship and with joy and gladness, devotedly engage themselves in magnifying the Name of Him Who is the Well-Beloved of all mankind. Verily He ordaineth according to His Own choosing. He hath now made interest on money lawful, even as He had made it unlawful in the past. Within His grasp He holdeth the kingdom of authority. He doeth and ordaineth. He is in truth the Ordainer, the All-Knowing.

Render thou thanks unto thy Lord, O Zaynu'l-Muqarrabín, for this manifest bounty.

[1] One of the early believers who is best known to the friends for his reliable transcriptions of the Tablets of Bahá'u'lláh. (See *Memorials of the Faithful* pp. 150–153.)

[2] Such loans as bear no interest and are repayable whenever the borrower pleases.

Many ecclesiastics in Persia have, through innumerable designs and devices, been feeding on illicit gains obtained by usury. They have contrived ways to give its outward form a fair semblance of lawfulness. They make a plaything of the laws and ordinances of God, but they understand not.

However, this is a matter that should be practised with moderation and fairness. Our Pen of Glory hath, as a token of wisdom and for the convenience of the people, desisted from laying down its limit. Nevertheless We exhort the loved ones of God to observe justice and fairness, and to do that which would prompt the friends of God to evince tender mercy and compassion towards each other. He is in truth the Counsellor, the Compassionate, the All-Bountiful. God grant that all men may be graciously aided to observe that which the Tongue of the One true God hath uttered. And if they put into practice what We have set forth, God—exalted be His glory—will assuredly double their portion through the heaven of His bounty. Verily He is the Generous, the Forgiving, the Compassionate. Praise be unto God, the Most Exalted, the Most Great.

Nevertheless the conduct of these affairs hath been entrusted to the men of the House of Justice that they may enforce them according to the exigencies of the time and the dictates of wisdom.

Once again We exhort all believers to observe justice and fairness and to show forth love and contentment. They are indeed the people of Bahá, the companions of the Crimson Ark. Upon them be the peace of God, the Lord of all Names, the Creator of the heavens.

9

LAWḤ-I-ḤIKMAT

(Tablet of Wisdom)

This Tablet was addressed to Áqá Muḥammad, a distin-guished believer from the town of Qá'in, who was surnamed Nabíl-i-Akbar (see Memorials of the Faithful *pages 1–5). Another distinguished believer of Qá'in, Mullá Muḥammad-'Alí, was known as Nabíl-i-Qá'iní (see* Memorials of the Faithful *pages 49–54). In the* abjad *notation the name 'Muḥammad' has the same numerical value as 'Nabíl'.*

THIS is an Epistle which the All-Merciful hath sent down from the Kingdom of Utterance. It is truly a breath of life unto those who dwell in the realm of creation. Glorified be the Lord of all worlds! In this Epistle mention is made of him who magnifieth the Name of God, his Lord, and who is named Nabíl in a weighty Tablet.

O Muhammad! Hearken unto the Voice proceeding out of the Realm of Glory, calling aloud from the celestial Tree which hath risen above the land of Za'farán[1]: Verily, no God is there but Me, the Omniscient, the Wise. Be thou as the breezes of the All-Merciful for the trees of the realm of existence and foster their growth through the potency of the Name of thy Lord, the Just, the All-Informed. We desire to acquaint thee with that which will serve as a reminder unto the people, that they may put away the things current amongst them and set their faces towards God, the Lord of the sincere.

We exhort mankind in these days when the countenance of Justice is soiled with dust, when the flames of unbelief are burning high and the robe of wisdom rent asunder, when tranquillity and faithfulness have ebbed away and

[1] In a Tablet Bahá'u'lláh states, 'The Holy Tree [Sadrat] is, in a sense, the Manifestation of the One True God, exalted be He. The Blessed Tree in the land of Za'farán referreth to the land which is flourishing, blessed, holy and all-perfumed, where that Tree hath been planted.'

trials and tribulations have waxed severe, when covenants are broken and ties are severed, when no man knoweth how to discern light and darkness or to distinguish guidance from error.

O peoples of the world! Forsake all evil, hold fast that which is good. Strive to be shining examples unto all mankind, and true reminders of the virtues of God amidst men. He that riseth to serve My Cause should manifest My wisdom, and bend every effort to banish ignorance from the earth. Be united in counsel, be one in thought. Let each morn be better than its eve and each morrow richer than its yesterday. Man's merit lieth in service and virtue and not in the pageantry of wealth and riches. Take heed that your words be purged from idle fancies and worldly desires and your deeds be cleansed from craftiness and suspicion. Dissipate not the wealth of your precious lives in the pursuit of evil and corrupt affection, nor let your endeavours be spent in promoting your personal interest. Be generous in your days of plenty, and be patient in the hour of loss. Adversity is followed by success and rejoicings follow woe. Guard against idleness and sloth, and cling unto that which profiteth mankind, whether young or old, whether high or low. Beware lest ye sow tares of dissension among men or plant thorns of doubt in pure and radiant hearts.

O ye beloved of the Lord! Commit not that which defileth the limpid stream of love or destroyeth the sweet fragrance of friendship. By the righteousness of the Lord! Ye were created to show love one to another and not perversity and rancour. Take pride not in love for yourselves but in love for your fellow-creatures. Glory not in love for your country, but in love for all mankind. Let your eye be chaste, your hand faithful, your tongue truthful and your heart enlightened. Abase not the station of the learned in Bahá and belittle not the rank of such rulers as administer justice amidst you. Set your reliance on the army of justice, put on the armour of wisdom, let your adorning be forgiveness and mercy and that which cheereth the hearts of the well-favoured of God.

By My life! Thy grievances have plunged Me into sorrow. Regard not the children of the world and all their doings but fix thy gaze upon God and His never-ending dominion. Verily, He calleth to thy remembrance that which is the source of delight for all mankind. Drink thou the life-giving water of blissful joy from the chalice of utterance proffered by the Fountainhead of divine Revelation—He Who hath made mention of thee in this mighty stronghold. Endeavour to the utmost of thy powers to establish the word of truth with eloquence and wisdom and to dispel falsehood from the face of the earth. Thus directeth thee the Dayspring of divine knowledge from this luminous horizon.

O thou who speakest in My Name! Consider the people and the things they have wrought in My days. We revealed unto one of the rulers that which overpowereth all the dwellers of the earth, and requested him to bring Us face to face with the learned men of this age, that We might set forth for him the testimony of God, His proofs, His glory and His majesty; and naught did We intend thereby but the highest good. However, he committed that which hath caused the inmates of the cities of justice and equity to lament. Thus hath judgement been given between Me and him. Verily thy Lord is the Ordainer, the All-Informed. In such circumstances as thou seest, how can the Celestial Bird soar into the atmosphere of divine mysteries when its wings have been battered with the stones of idle fancy and bitter hatred, and it is cast into a prison built of unyielding stone? By the righteousness of God! The people have perpetrated a grievous injustice.

As regards thine assertions about the beginning of creation, this is a matter on which conceptions vary by reason of the divergences in men's thoughts and opinions. Wert thou to assert that it hath ever existed and shall continue to exist, it would be true; or wert thou to affirm the same concept as is mentioned in the sacred Scriptures, no doubt would there be about it, for it hath been revealed by God, the Lord of the worlds. Indeed He was a hidden treasure. This is a station that can never be described nor even alluded to. And in the station of 'I did wish to make Myself known', God was, and His creation had ever existed beneath His shelter from the beginning that hath no beginning, apart from its being preceded by a Firstness which cannot be regarded as firstness and originated by a Cause inscrutable even unto all men of learning.

That which hath been in existence had existed before, but not in the form thou seest today. The world of existence came into being through the heat generated from the interaction between the active force and that which is its recipient. These two are the same, yet they are different. Thus doth the Great Announcement inform thee about this glorious structure. Such as communicate the generating influence and such as receive its impact are indeed created through the irresistible Word of God which is the Cause of the entire creation, while all else besides His Word are but the creatures and the effects thereof. Verily thy Lord is the Expounder, the All-Wise.

Know thou, moreover, that the Word of God—exalted be His glory—is higher and far superior to that which the senses can perceive, for it is sanctified from any property or substance. It transcendeth the limitations of known elements and is exalted above all the essential and recognized substances. It became manifest without any syllable or sound and is none but the Command of God which pervadeth all created things. It hath never been withheld from the world of being. It is God's all-pervasive grace, from which all grace doth emanate. It is an entity far removed above all that hath been and shall be.

We are loath to enlarge on this subject, inasmuch as the unbelievers have inclined their ears towards Us in order to hear that which might enable them to cavil against God, the Help in Peril, the Self-Subsisting. And since they are unable to attain to mysteries of knowledge and wisdom from what hath been unravelled by the Source of divine splendour, they rise in protest and burst into clamour. But it is true to say that they object to that which they comprehend, not to the expositions given by the Expounder, nor the truths imparted by the One true God, the Knower of things unseen. Their objections, one and all, turn upon themselves, and I swear by thy life that they are devoid of understanding.

Every thing must needs have an origin and every building a builder. Verily, the Word of God is the Cause which hath preceded the contingent world—a world which is adorned with the splendours of the Ancient of Days, yet is being renewed and regenerated at all times. Immeasurably exalted is the God of Wisdom Who hath raised this sublime structure.

Look at the world and ponder a while upon it. It unveileth the book of its own self before thine eyes and revealeth that which the Pen of thy Lord, the Fashioner, the All-Informed, hath inscribed therein. It will acquaint thee with that which is within it and upon it and will give thee such clear explanations as to make thee independent of every eloquent expounder.

Say: Nature in its essence is the embodiment of My Name, the Maker, the Creator. Its manifestations are diversified by varying causes, and in this diversity there are signs for men of discernment. Nature is God's Will and is its expression in and through the contingent world. It is a dispensation of Providence ordained by the Ordainer, the All-Wise. Were anyone to affirm that it is the Will of God as manifested in the world of being, no one should question this assertion. It is endowed with a power whose reality men of learning fail to grasp. Indeed a man of insight can perceive naught therein save the effulgent splendour of Our Name, the Creator. Say: This is an existence which knoweth no decay, and Nature itself is lost in bewilderment before its revelations, its compelling evidences and its effulgent glory which have encompassed the universe.

It ill beseemeth thee to turn thy gaze unto former or more recent times. Make thou mention of this Day and magnify that which hath appeared therein. It will in truth suffice all mankind. Indeed expositions and discourses in explanation of such things cause the spirits to be chilled. It behoveth thee to speak forth in such wise as to set the hearts of true believers ablaze and cause their bodies to soar.

Whoso firmly believeth today in the rebirth of man and is fully conscious that God, the Most Exalted, wieldeth supreme ascendancy and absolute authority over this new creation, verily such a man is reckoned with them that are endued with insight in this most great Revelation. Unto this beareth witness every discerning believer.

Walk thou high above the world of being through the power of the Most Great Name, that thou mayest become aware of the immemorial mysteries and be acquainted with that wherewith no one is acquainted. Verily, thy Lord is the Helper, the All-Knowing, the All-Informed. Be thou as a throbbing artery, pulsating in the body of the entire creation, that through the heat generated by this motion there may appear that which will quicken the hearts of those who hesitate.

At the time when We were hidden behind countless veils of light thou didst commune with Me and didst witness the luminaries of the heaven of My wisdom and the billows of the ocean of Mine utterance. Verily thy Lord is the Truthful, the Faithful. Great indeed is the blessedness of him who hath attained the liberal effusions of this ocean in the days of his Lord, the Most Bountiful, the All-Wise.

During Our sojourn in 'Iráq when We were at the house of one named Majíd, We set forth clearly for thee the mysteries of creation and the origin, the culmination and the cause thereof. However since Our departure We have limited Ourself to this affirmation: 'Verily, no God is there but Me, the Ever-Forgiving, the Bountiful.'

Teach thou the Cause of God with an utterance which will cause the bushes to be enkindled, and the call 'Verily, there is no God but Me, the Almighty, the Unconstrained' to be raised therefrom. Say: Human utterance is an essence which aspireth to exert its influence and needeth moderation. As to its influence, this is conditional upon refinement which in turn is dependent upon hearts which are detached and pure. As to its moderation, this hath to be combined with tact and wisdom as prescribed in the Holy Scriptures and Tablets. Meditate upon that which hath streamed forth from the heaven of the Will of thy Lord, He Who is the Source of all grace, that thou mayest grasp the intended meaning which is enshrined in the sacred depths of the Holy Writings.

Those who have rejected God and firmly cling to

Nature as it is in itself are, verily, bereft of knowledge and wisdom. They are truly of them that are far astray. They have failed to attain the lofty summit and have fallen short of the ultimate purpose; therefore their eyes were shut and their thoughts differed, while the leaders among them have believed in God and in His invincible sovereignty. Unto this beareth witness thy Lord, the Help in Peril, the Self-Subsisting.

When the eyes of the people of the East were captivated by the arts and wonders of the West, they roved distraught in the wilderness of material causes, oblivious of the One Who is the Causer of Causes, and the Sustainer thereof, while such men as were the source and the wellspring of Wisdom never denied the moving Impulse behind these causes, nor the Creator or the Origin thereof. Thy Lord knoweth, yet most of the people know not.

Now We have, for the sake of God, the Lord of Names, set Ourself the task of mentioning in this Tablet some accounts of the sages,[1] that the eyes of the people may be opened thereby and that they may become fully assured that He is in truth the Maker, the Omnipotent, the Creator, the Originator, the All-Knowing, the All-Wise.

Although it is recognized that the contemporary men of learning are highly qualified in philosophy, arts and crafts, yet were anyone to observe with a discriminating eye he would readily comprehend that most of this knowledge hath been acquired from the sages of the past, for it is they who have laid the foundation of philosophy, reared its structure and reinforced its pillars. Thus doth thy Lord, the Ancient of Days, inform thee. The sages aforetime acquired

---

[1] In many of the passages that follow concerning the Greek philosophers, Bahá'u'lláh quotes verbatim from the works of such Muslim historians as Abu'l-Fatḥ-i-Shahristání (1076–1153 A.D.) and 'Imádu'd-Dín Abu'l-Fidá (1273–1331 A.D.).

their knowledge from the Prophets, inasmuch as the latter were the Exponents of divine philosophy and the Revealers of heavenly mysteries. Men quaffed the crystal, living waters of Their utterance, while others satisfied themselves with the dregs. Everyone receiveth a portion according to his measure. Verily He is the Equitable, the Wise.

Empedocles, who distinguished himself in philosophy, was a contemporary of David, while Pythagoras lived in the days of Solomon, son of David, and acquired Wisdom from the treasury of prophethood. It is he who claimed to have heard the whispering sound of the heavens and to have attained the station of the angels. In truth thy Lord will clearly set forth all things, if He pleaseth. Verily, He is the Wise, the All-Pervading.

The essence and the fundamentals of philosophy have emanated from the Prophets. That the people differ concerning the inner meanings and mysteries thereof is to be attributed to the divergence of their views and minds. We would fain recount to thee the following: One of the Prophets once was communicating to his people that with which the Omnipotent Lord had inspired Him. Truly, thy Lord is the Inspirer, the Gracious, the Exalted. When the fountain of wisdom and eloquence gushed forth from the wellspring of His utterance and the wine of divine knowledge inebriated those who had sought His threshold, He exclaimed: 'Lo! All are filled with the Spirit.' From among the people there was he who held fast unto this statement and, actuated by his own fancies, conceived the idea that the spirit literally penetrateth or entereth into the body, and through lengthy expositions he advanced proofs to vindicate this concept; and groups of people followed in his footsteps. To mention their names at this point, or to give thee a detailed account thereof, would lead to prolixity, and would depart from the main theme. Verily, thy Lord is the

All-Wise, the All-Knowing. There was also he who partook of the choice wine whose seal had been removed by the Key of the Tongue of Him Who is the Revealer of the Verses of thy Lord, the Gracious, the Most Generous.

Verily, the philosophers have not denied the Ancient of Days. Most of them passed away deploring their failure to fathom His mystery, even as some of them have testified. Verily, thy Lord is the Adviser, the All-Informed.

Consider Hippocrates, the physician. He was one of the eminent philosophers who believed in God and acknowledged His sovereignty. After him came Socrates who was indeed wise, accomplished and righteous. He practised self-denial, repressed his appetites for selfish desires and turned away from material pleasures. He withdrew to the mountains where he dwelt in a cave. He dissuaded men from worshipping idols and taught them the way of God, the Lord of Mercy, until the ignorant rose up against him. They arrested him and put him to death in prison. Thus relateth to thee this swift-moving Pen. What a penetrating vision into philosophy this eminent man had! He is the most distinguished of all philosophers and was highly versed in wisdom. We testify that he is one of the heroes in this field and an outstanding champion dedicated unto it. He had a profound knowledge of such sciences as were current amongst men as well as of those which were veiled from their minds. Methinks he drank one draught when the Most Great Ocean overflowed with gleaming and life-giving waters. He it is who perceived a unique, a tempered, and a pervasive nature in things, bearing the closest likeness to the human spirit, and he discovered this nature to be distinct from the substance of things in their refined form. He hath a special pronouncement on this weighty theme. Wert thou to ask from the worldly wise of this generation about this exposition, thou wouldst witness their incapacity to grasp it. Verily, thy Lord speaketh the truth but most people comprehend not.

After Socrates came the divine Plato who was a pupil of the former and occupied the chair of philosophy as his successor. He acknowledged his belief in God and in His signs which pervade all that hath been and shall be. Then came Aristotle, the well-known man of knowledge. He it is who discovered the power of gaseous matter. These men who stand out as leaders of the people and are pre-eminent among them, one and all acknowledged their belief in the immortal Being Who holdeth in His grasp the reins of all sciences.

I will also mention for thee the invocation voiced by Balínús who was familiar with the theories put forward by the Father of Philosophy regarding the mysteries of creation as given in his chrysolite tablets, that everyone may be fully assured of the things We have elucidated for thee in this manifest Tablet, which, if pressed with the hand of fairness and knowledge, will yield the spirit of life for the quickening of all created things. Great is the blessedness of him who swimmeth in this ocean and celebrateth the praise of his Lord, the Gracious, the Best-Beloved. Indeed the breezes of divine revelation are diffused from the verses of thy Lord in such wise that no one can dispute its truth, except those who are bereft of hearing, of vision, of understanding and of every human faculty. Verily thy Lord beareth witness unto this, yet the people understand not.

This man hath said: 'I am Balínús, the wise one, the performer of wonders, the producer of talismans.' He surpassed everyone else in the diffusion of arts and sciences and soared unto the loftiest heights of humility and supplication. Give ear unto that which he hath said, entreating the

All-Possessing, the Most Exalted: 'I stand in the presence of my Lord, extolling His gifts and bounties and praising Him with that wherewith He praiseth His Own Self, that I may become a source of blessing and guidance unto such men as acknowledge my words.' And further he saith: 'O Lord! Thou art God and no God is there but Thee. Thou art the Creator and no creator is there except Thee. Assist me by Thy grace and strengthen me. My heart is seized with alarm, my limbs tremble, I have lost my reason and my mind hath failed me. Bestow upon me strength and enable my tongue to speak forth with wisdom.' And still further he saith: 'Thou art in truth the Knowing, the Wise, the Powerful, the Compassionate.' It was this man of wisdom who became informed of the mysteries of creation and discerned the subtleties which lie enshrined in the Hermetic writings.[1]

We have no wish to mention anything further but We shall utter that which the Spirit hath instilled into My heart. In truth there is no God but Him, the Knowing, the Mighty, the Help in Peril, the Most Excellent, the All-Praised. By My life! In this Day the celestial Tree is loath to proclaim aught else to the world but this affirmation:

---

[1] In one of His Tablets Bahá'u'lláh wrote: 'The first person who devoted himself to philosophy was Idrís. Thus was he named. Some called him also Hermes. In every tongue he hath a special name. He it is who hath set forth in every branch of philosophy thorough and convincing statements. After him Balínús derived his knowledge and sciences from the Hermetic Tablets and most of the philosophers who followed him made their philosophical and scientific discoveries from his words and statements . . .'. In the Qur'án, Súra 19, verses 57 and 58, is written: 'And commemorate Idrís in the Book; for he was a man of truth, a Prophet; And we uplifted him to a place on high.'

'Verily, there is none other God but Me, the Peerless, the All-Informed.'

Had it not been for the love I cherish for thee, I would not have uttered a single word of what hath been mentioned. Appreciate the value of this station and preserve it as thou wouldst thine eye and be of them that are truly thankful.

Thou knowest full well that We perused not the books which men possess and We acquired not the learning current amongst them, and yet whenever We desire to quote the sayings of the learned and of the wise,[1] presently there will appear before the face of thy Lord in the form of a tablet all that which hath appeared in the world and is revealed in the Holy Books and Scriptures. Thus do We set down in writing that which the eye perceiveth. Verily His knowledge encompasseth the earth and the heavens.

This is a Tablet wherein the Pen of the Unseen hath inscribed the knowledge of all that hath been and shall be— a knowledge that none other but My wondrous Tongue can interpret. Indeed My heart as it is in itself hath been purged by God from the concepts of the learned and is sanctified from the utterances of the wise. In truth naught doth it mirror forth but the revelations of God. Unto this beareth witness the Tongue of Grandeur in this perspicuous Book.

Say, O people of the earth! Beware lest any reference to wisdom debar you from its Source or withhold you from the Dawning-Place thereof. Fix your hearts upon your Lord, the Educator, the All-Wise.

For every land We have prescribed a portion, for every occasion an allotted share, for every pronouncement an appointed time and for every situation an apt remark. Consider Greece. We made it a Seat of Wisdom for a prolonged

[1] See footnote on p. 144.

period. However, when the appointed hour struck, its throne was subverted, its tongue ceased to speak, its light grew dim and its banner was hauled down. Thus do We bestow and withdraw. Verily thy Lord is He Who giveth and divesteth, the Mighty, the Powerful.

In every land We have set up a luminary of knowledge, and when the time foreordained is at hand, it will shine resplendent above its horizon, as decreed by God, the All-Knowing, the All-Wise. If it be Our Will We are fully capable of describing for thee whatever existeth in every land or hath come to pass therein. Indeed the knowledge of thy Lord pervadeth the heavens and the earth.

Know thou, moreover, that the people aforetime have produced things which the contemporary men of knowledge have been unable to produce. We recall unto thee Múrṭus who was one of the learned. He invented an apparatus which transmitted sound over a distance of sixty miles. Others besides him have also discovered things which no one in this age hath beheld. Verily thy Lord revealeth in every epoch whatsoever He pleaseth as a token of wisdom on His part. He is in truth the supreme Ordainer, the All-Wise.

A true philosopher would never deny God nor His evidences, rather would he acknowledge His glory and overpowering majesty which overshadow all created things. Verily We love those men of knowledge who have brought to light such things as promote the best interests of humanity, and We aided them through the potency of Our behest, for well are We able to achieve Our purpose.

Beware, O My loved ones, lest ye despise the merits of My learned servants whom God hath graciously chosen to be the exponents of His Name 'the Fashioner' amidst mankind. Exert your utmost endeavour that ye may develop such crafts and undertakings that everyone, whether young or old, may benefit therefrom. We are quit of those ignorant ones who fondly imagine that Wisdom is to give vent to one's idle imaginings and to repudiate God, the Lord of all men; even as We hear some of the heedless voicing such assertions today.

Say: The beginning of Wisdom and the origin thereof is to acknowledge whatsoever God hath clearly set forth, for through its potency the foundation of statesmanship, which is a shield for the preservation of the body of mankind, hath been firmly established. Ponder a while that ye may perceive what My most exalted Pen hath proclaimed in this wondrous Tablet. Say, every matter related to state affairs which ye raise for discussion falls under the shadow of one of the words sent down from the heaven of His glorious and exalted utterance. Thus have We recounted unto thee that which will exhilarate thy heart, will bring solace to thine eyes and will enable thee to arise for the promotion of His Cause amidst all peoples.

O My Nabíl! Let nothing grieve thee, rather rejoice with exceeding gladness inasmuch as I have mentioned thy name, have turned My heart and My face towards thee and have conversed with thee through this irrefutable and weighty exposition. Ponder in thy heart upon the tribulations I have sustained, the imprisonment and the captivity I have endured, the sufferings that have befallen Me and the accusations that the people have levelled against Me. Behold, they are truly wrapped in a grievous veil.

When the discourse reached this stage, the dawn of divine mysteries appeared and the light of utterance was quenched. May His glory rest upon the people of wisdom as bidden by One Who is the Almighty, the All-Praised.

Say: Magnified be Thy Name, O Lord my God! I

beseech Thee by Thy Name through which the splendour of the light of wisdom shone resplendent when the heavens of divine utterance were set in motion amidst mankind, to graciously aid me by Thy heavenly confirmations and enable me to extol Thy Name amongst Thy servants.

O Lord! Unto Thee have I turned my face, detached from all save Thee and holding fast to the hem of the robe of Thy manifold blessings. Unloose my tongue therefore to proclaim that which will captivate the minds of men and will rejoice their souls and spirits. Strengthen me then in Thy Cause in such wise that I may not be hindered by the ascendancy of the oppressors among Thy creatures nor withheld by the onslaught of the disbelievers amidst those who dwell in Thy realm. Make me as a lamp shining throughout Thy lands that those in whose hearts the light of Thy knowledge gloweth and the yearning for Thy love lingereth may be guided by its radiance.

Verily, potent art Thou to do whatsoever Thou willest, and in Thy grasp Thou holdest the kingdom of creation. There is none other God but Thee, the Almighty, the All-Wise.

10

AṢL-I-KULLU'L-KHAYR

(Words of Wisdom)

In the Name of God, the Exalted, the Most High

THE source of all good is trust in God, submission unto His command, and contentment with His holy will and pleasure.

The essence of wisdom is the fear of God, the dread of His scourge and punishment, and the apprehension of His justice and decree.

The essence of religion is to testify unto that which the Lord hath revealed, and follow that which He hath ordained in His mighty Book.

The source of all glory is acceptance of whatsoever the Lord hath bestowed, and contentment with that which God hath ordained.

The essence of love is for man to turn his heart to the Beloved One, and sever himself from all else but Him, and desire naught save that which is the desire of his Lord.

True remembrance is to make mention of the Lord, the All-Praised, and forget aught else beside Him.

True reliance is for the servant to pursue his profession and calling in this world, to hold fast unto the Lord, to seek naught but His grace, inasmuch as in His Hands is the destiny of all His servants.

The essence of detachment is for man to turn his face towards the courts of the Lord, to enter His Presence, behold His Countenance, and stand as witness before Him.

The essence of understanding is to testify to one's

poverty, and submit to the Will of the Lord, the Sovereign, the Gracious, the All-Powerful.

The source of courage and power is the promotion of the Word of God, and steadfastness in His Love.

The essence of charity is for the servant to recount the blessings of his Lord, and to render thanks unto Him at all times and under all conditions.

The essence of faith is fewness of words and abundance of deeds; he whose words exceed his deeds, know verily his death is better than his life.

The essence of true safety is to observe silence, to look at the end of things and to renounce the world.

The beginning of magnanimity is when man expendeth his wealth on himself, on his family and on the poor among his brethren in his Faith.

The essence of wealth is love for Me; whoso loveth Me is the possessor of all things, and he that loveth Me not is indeed of the poor and needy. This is that which the Finger of Glory and Splendour hath revealed.

The source of all evil is for man to turn away from his Lord and set his heart on things ungodly.

The most burning fire is to question the signs of God, to dispute idly that which He hath revealed, to deny Him and carry one's self proudly before Him.

The source of all learning is the knowledge of God, exalted be His Glory, and this cannot be attained save through the knowledge of His Divine Manifestation.

The essence of abasement is to pass out from under the shadow of the Merciful and seek the shelter of the Evil One.

The source of error is to disbelieve in the One true God, rely upon aught else but Him, and flee from His Decree.

True loss is for him whose days have been spent in utter ignorance of his self.

The essence of all that We have revealed for thee is Justice, is for man to free himself from idle fancy and imitation, discern with the eye of oneness His glorious handiwork, and look into all things with a searching eye.

Thus have We instructed thee, manifested unto thee Words of Wisdom, that thou mayest be thankful unto the Lord, thy God, and glory therein amidst all peoples.

11

LAWḤ-I-MAQṢÚD
(Tablet of Maqṣúd)

Out of respect, the Bahá'ís, rather than addressing Bahá'u'lláh directly, would write to His amanuensis, Mírzá Áqá Ján, surnamed 'Servant of God' and 'Servant-in-Attendance'. The reply would be in the form of a letter from Mírzá Áqá Ján quoting words of Bahá'u'lláh, but would, in fact, be dictated in its entirety by Bahá'u'lláh. Thus all parts of the Tablet, even those which ostensibly are the words of Mírzá Áqá Ján himself, are Sacred Scripture revealed by Bahá'u'lláh. The Tablet of Maqṣúd is in this form. It was addressed to Mírzá Maqṣúd, one of the early believers living at that time in Damascus and Jerusalem.

PRAISE which is exalted above every mention or description beseemeth the Adored One, the Possessor of all things visible and invisible, Who hath enabled the Primal Point to reveal countless Books and Epistles and Who, through the potency of His sublime Word, hath called into being the entire creation, whether of the former or more recent generations. Moreover He hath in every age and cycle, in conformity with His transcendent wisdom, sent forth a divine Messenger to revive the dispirited and despondent souls with the living waters of His utterance, One Who is indeed the Expounder, the true Interpreter, inasmuch as man is unable to comprehend that which hath streamed forth from the Pen of Glory and is recorded in His heavenly Books. Men at all times and under all conditions stand in need of one to exhort them, guide them and to instruct and teach them. Therefore He hath sent forth His Messengers, His Prophets and chosen ones that they might acquaint the people with the divine purpose underlying the revelation of Books and the raising up of Messengers, and that everyone may become aware of the trust of God which is latent in the reality of every soul.

Man is the supreme Talisman. Lack of a proper education hath, however, deprived him of that which he doth inherently possess. Through a word proceeding out of the mouth of God he was called into being; by one word more he was guided to recognize the Source of his education; by yet another word his station and destiny were safeguarded. The Great Being saith: Regard man as a mine rich in gems of inestimable value. Education can, alone, cause it to reveal its treasures, and enable mankind to benefit there-from. If any man were to meditate on that which the Scriptures, sent down from the heaven of God's holy Will, have revealed, he would readily recognize that their purpose is that all men shall be regarded as one soul, so that the seal bearing the words 'The Kingdom shall be God's' may be stamped on every heart, and the light of Divine bounty, of grace, and mercy may envelop all mankind. The One true God, exalted be His glory, hath wished nothing for Him-self. The allegiance of mankind profiteth Him not, neither doth its perversity harm Him. The Bird of the Realm of Utterance voiceth continually this call: 'All things have I willed for thee, and thee, too, for thine own sake.' If the learned and worldly-wise men of this age were to allow mankind to inhale the fragrance of fellowship and love, every understanding heart would apprehend the meaning of true liberty, and discover the secret of undisturbed peace and absolute composure. Were the earth to attain this station and be illumined with its light it could then be truly said of it: 'Thou shall see in it no hollows or rising hills.'[1]

Blessing and peace be upon Him[2] through Whose advent Baṭḥá[3] is wreathed in smiles, and the sweet savours of Whose raiment have shed fragrance upon all mankind— He Who came to protect men from that which would harm them in the world below. Exalted, immensely

[1] Qur'án 20:106.
[2] Muḥammad.
[3] Mecca.

exalted is His station above the glorification of all beings and sanctified from the praise of the entire creation. Through His advent the tabernacle of stability and order was raised throughout the world and the ensign of knowledge hoisted among the nations. May blessings rest also upon His kindred and His companions through whom the standard of the unity of God and of His singleness was uplifted and the banners of celestial triumph were unfurled. Through them the religion of God was firmly established among His creatures and His Name magnified amidst His servants. I entreat Him—exalted is He—to shield His Faith from the mischief of His enemies who tore away the veils, rent them asunder and finally caused the banner of Islám to be reversed amongst all peoples.

Thy letter from which the fragrance of reunion was inhaled hath been received. Praised be God that following the firm decree of separation, the breeze of nearness and communion hath been stirred and the soil of the heart is refreshed with the waters of joy and gladness. We offer thanksgiving unto God in all circumstances and cherish the hope that He—exalted be His glory—may through His gracious providence guide all who dwell on earth towards that which is acceptable and pleasing unto Him.

Behold the disturbances which, for many a long year, have afflicted the earth, and the perturbation that hath seized its peoples. It hath either been ravaged by war, or tormented by sudden and unforeseen calamities. Though the world is encompassed with misery and distress, yet no man hath paused to reflect what the cause or source of that may be. Whenever the True Counsellor uttered a word in admonishment, lo, they all denounced Him as a mover of mischief and rejected His claim. How bewildering, how confusing is such behaviour! No two men can be found who may be said to be outwardly and inwardly united. The evidences of discord and malice are apparent everywhere, though all were made for harmony and union. The Great Being saith: O well-beloved ones! The tabernacle of unity hath been raised; regard ye not one another as strangers. Ye are the fruits of one tree, and the leaves of one branch. We cherish the hope that the light of justice may shine upon the world and sanctify it from tyranny. If the rulers and kings of the earth, the symbols of the power of God, exalted be His glory, arise and resolve to dedicate themselves to whatever will promote the highest interests of the whole of humanity, the reign of justice will assuredly be established amongst the children of men, and the effulgence of its light will envelop the whole earth. The Great Being saith: The structure of world stability and order hath been reared upon, and will continue to be sustained by, the twin pillars of reward and punishment. And in another connection He hath uttered the following in the eloquent tongue:[1] Justice hath a mighty force at its command. It is none other than reward and punishment for the deeds of men. By the power of this force the tabernacle of order is established throughout the world, causing the wicked to restrain their natures for fear of punishment.

In another passage He hath written: Take heed, O concourse of the rulers of the world! There is no force on earth that can equal in its conquering power the force of justice and wisdom. I, verily, affirm that there is not, and hath never been, a host more mighty than that of justice and wisdom. Blessed is the king who marcheth with the ensign of wisdom unfurled before him, and the battalions of justice massed in his rear. He verily is the ornament that adorneth the brow of peace and the countenance of

[1] Arabic.

security. There can be no doubt whatever that if the day-star of justice, which the clouds of tyranny have obscured, were to shed its light upon men, the face of the earth would be completely transformed.

The Great Being, wishing to reveal the prerequisites of the peace and tranquillity of the world and the advance-ment of its peoples, hath written: The time must come when the imperative necessity for the holding of a vast, an all-embracing assemblage of men will be universally realized. The rulers and kings of the earth must needs attend it, and, participating in its deliberations, must con-sider such ways and means as will lay the foundations of the world's Great Peace amongst men. Such a peace demandeth that the Great Powers should resolve, for the sake of the tranquillity of the peoples of the earth, to be fully reconciled among themselves. Should any king take up arms against another, all should unitedly arise and prevent him. If this be done, the nations of the world will no longer require any armaments, except for the purpose of preserving the security of their realms and of maintaining internal order within their territories. This will ensure the peace and com-posure of every people, government and nation. We fain would hope that the kings and rulers of the earth, the mirrors of the gracious and almighty name of God, may attain unto this station, and shield mankind from the on-slaught of tyranny.

Likewise He saith: Among the things which are con-ducive to unity and concord and will cause the whole earth to be regarded as one country is that the divers languages be reduced to one language and in like manner the scripts used in the world be confined to a single script. It is incumbent upon all nations to appoint some men of understanding and erudition to convene a gathering and through joint consultation choose one language from among the varied existing languages, or create a new one, to be taught to the children in all the schools of the world.

The day is approaching when all the peoples of the world will have adopted one universal language and one common script. When this is achieved, to whatsoever city a man may journey, it shall be as if he were entering his own home. These things are obligatory and absolutely essential. It is incumbent upon every man of insight and understanding to strive to translate that which hath been written into reality and action.

In these days the tabernacle of justice hath fallen into the clutches of tyranny and oppression. Beseech ye the One true God—exalted be His glory—not to deprive mankind of the ocean of true understanding, for were men but to take heed they would readily appreciate that whatever hath streamed from and is set down by the Pen of Glory is even as the sun for the whole world and that therein lie the welfare, security and true interests of all men; otherwise the earth will be tormented by a fresh calamity every day and unprecedented commotions will break out. God grant that the people of the world may be graciously aided to preserve the light of His loving counsels within the globe of wisdom. We cherish the hope that everyone may be adorned with the vesture of true wisdom, the basis of the government of the world.

The Great Being saith: The heaven of statesmanship is made luminous and resplendent by the brightness of the light of these blessed words which hath dawned from the dayspring of the Will of God: It behoveth every ruler to weigh his own being every day in the balance of equity and justice and then to judge between men and counsel them to do that which would direct their steps unto the path of wisdom and understanding. This is the cornerstone of statesmanship and the essence thereof. From these words every enlightened man of wisdom will readily perceive that which will foster such aims as the welfare, security and protection of mankind and the safety of human lives. Were men of insight to quaff their fill from the ocean of inner meanings which lie enshrined in these words and become acquainted therewith, they would bear witness to the sublimity and the excellence of this utterance. If this lowly one were to set forth that which he perceiveth, all would testify unto God's consummate wisdom. The secrets of statesmanship and that of which the people are in need lie enfolded within these words. This lowly servant earnestly entreateth the One true God—exalted be His glory—to illumine the eyes of the people of the world with the splendour of the light of wisdom that they, one and all, may recognize that which is indispensable in this day.

That one indeed is a man who, today, dedicateth himself to the service of the entire human race. The Great Being saith: Blessed and happy is he that ariseth to promote the best interests of the peoples and kindreds of the earth. In another passage He hath proclaimed: It is not for him to pride himself who loveth his own country, but rather for him who loveth the whole world. The earth is but one country, and mankind its citizens.

Such exhortations to union and concord as are inscribed in the Books of the Prophets by the Pen of the Most High bear reference unto specific matters; not a union that would lead to disunity or a concord which would create discord. This is the station where measures are set unto everything, a station where every deserving soul shall be given his due. Well is it with them that appreciate the meaning and grasp the intent of these words, and woe betide the heedless. Unto this all the evidences of nature, in their very essences, bear ample testimony. Every discerning man of wisdom is well acquainted with that which We have mentioned, but not those who have strayed far from the living fountain of fairmindedness and are roving distraught in the wilderness of ignorance and blind fanaticism.

The Great Being saith: O ye children of men! The fundamental purpose animating the Faith of God and His Religion is to safeguard the interests and promote the unity of the human race, and to foster the spirit of love and fellowship amongst men. Suffer it not to become a source of dissension and discord, of hate and enmity. This is the straight Path, the fixed and immovable foundation. Whatsoever is raised on this foundation, the changes and chances of the world can never impair its strength, nor will the revolution of countless centuries undermine its structure. Our hope is that the world's religious leaders and the rulers thereof will unitedly arise for the reformation of this age and the rehabilitation of its fortunes. Let them, after meditating on its needs, take counsel together and, through anxious and full deliberation, administer to a diseased and sorely-afflicted world the remedy it requireth.

The Great Being saith: The heaven of divine wisdom is illumined with the two luminaries of consultation and compassion. Take ye counsel together in all matters, inasmuch as consultation is the lamp of guidance which leadeth the way, and is the bestower of understanding.

At the outset of every endeavour, it is incumbent to look to the end of it. Of all the arts and sciences, set the children to studying those which will result in advantage to man, will ensure his progress and elevate his rank. Thus the noisome odours of lawlessness will be dispelled, and thus through the high endeavours of the nation's leaders, all will live cradled, secure and in peace.

The Great Being saith: The learned of the day must direct the people to acquire those branches of knowledge which are of use, that both the learned themselves and the generality of mankind may derive benefits therefrom. Such academic pursuits as begin and end in words alone have never been and will never be of any worth. The majority of Persia's learned doctors devote all their lives to the study of a philosophy the ultimate yield of which is nothing but words.

It is incumbent upon them who are in authority to exercise moderation in all things. Whatsoever passeth beyond the limits of moderation will cease to exert a beneficial influence. Consider for instance such things as liberty, civilization and the like. However much men of understanding may favourably regard them, they will, if carried to excess, exercise a pernicious influence upon men.

If this point were to be expounded an elaborate explanation would be required which, it is feared, might become tedious. It is the ardent hope of this lowly one that God—exalted be His glory—may grant all men that which is good. For he who is endowed therewith is the possessor of all things. The Great Being saith: The Tongue of Wisdom proclaimeth: He that hath Me not is bereft of all things. Turn ye away from all that is on earth and seek none else but Me. I am the Sun of Wisdom and the Ocean of Knowledge. I cheer the faint and revive the dead. I am the guiding Light that illumineth the way. I am the royal Falcon on the arm of the Almighty. I unfold the drooping wings of every broken bird and start it on its flight.

And likewise He saith: The heaven of true understanding

shineth resplendent with the light of two luminaries: tolerance and righteousness.

O my friend! Vast oceans lie enshrined within this brief saying. Blessed are they who appreciate its value, drink deep therefrom and grasp its meaning, and woe betide the heedless. This lowly one entreateth the people of the world to observe fairness, that their tender, their delicate and precious hearing which hath been created to hearken unto the words of wisdom may be freed from impediments and from such allusions, idle fancies or vain imaginings as 'cannot fatten nor appease the hunger', so that the true Counsellor may be graciously inclined to set forth that which is the source of blessing for mankind and of the highest good for all nations.

At present the light of reconciliation is dimmed in most countries and its radiance extinguished while the fire of strife and disorder hath been kindled and is blazing fiercely. Two great powers who regard themselves as the founders and leaders of civilization and the framers of constitutions have risen up against the followers of the Faith associated with Him Who conversed with God.[1] Be ye warned, O men of understanding. It ill beseemeth the station of man to commit tyranny; rather it behoveth him to observe equity and be attired with the raiment of justice under all conditions. Beseech ye the One true God that He may, through the power of the hand of loving-kindness and spiritual education, purge and purify certain souls from the defilement of evil passions and corrupt desires, that they may arise and unloose their tongues for the sake of God, that perchance the evidences of injustice may be blotted out and the splendour of the light of justice may shed its radiance upon the whole world. The people are ignorant,

[1] Moses.

and they stand in need of those who will expound the truth.

The Great Being saith: The man of consummate learning and the sage endowed with penetrating wisdom are the two eyes to the body of mankind. God willing, the earth shall never be deprived of these two greatest gifts. That which hath been set forth and will be revealed in the future is but a token of this Servant's ardent desire to dedicate Himself to the service of all the kindreds of the earth.

O my friend! In all circumstances one should seize upon every means which will promote security and tranquillity among the peoples of the world. The Great Being saith: In this glorious Day whatever will purge you from corruption and will lead you towards peace and composure, is indeed the Straight Path.

Please God, the peoples of the world may be led, as the result of the high endeavours exerted by their rulers and the wise and learned amongst men, to recognize their best interests. How long will humanity persist in its wayward-ness? How long will injustice continue? How long is chaos and confusion to reign amongst men? How long will discord agitate the face of society?

This humble servant is filled with wonder, inasmuch as all men are endowed with the capacity to see and hear, yet we find them deprived of the privilege of using these faculties. This servant hath been prompted to pen these lines by virtue of the tender love he cherisheth for thee. The winds of despair are, alas, blowing from every direction, and the strife that divideth and afflicteth the human race is daily increasing. The signs of impending convulsions and chaos can now be discerned, inasmuch as the prevailing order appeareth to be lamentably defective. I beseech God, exalted be His glory, that He may graciously awaken the peoples of the earth, may grant that the end of their conduct may be profitable unto them, and aid them to accomplish that which beseemeth their station.

Were man to appreciate the greatness of his station and the loftiness of his destiny he would manifest naught save goodly character, pure deeds, and a seemly and praiseworthy conduct. If the learned and wise men of goodwill were to impart guidance unto the people, the whole earth would be regarded as one country. Verily this is the undoubted truth. This servant appealeth to every diligent and enterprising soul to exert his utmost endeavour and arise to rehabilitate the conditions in all regions and to quicken the dead with the living waters of wisdom and utterance, by virtue of the love he cherisheth for God, the One, the Peerless, the Almighty, the Beneficent.

No man of wisdom can demonstrate his knowledge save by means of words. This showeth the significance of the Word as is affirmed in all the Scriptures, whether of former times or more recently. For it is through its potency and animating spirit that the people of the world have attained so eminent a position. Moreover words and utterances should be both impressive and penetrating. However, no word will be infused with these two qualities unless it be uttered wholly for the sake of God and with due regard unto the exigencies of the occasion and the people.

The Great Being saith: Human utterance is an essence which aspireth to exert its influence and needeth moderation. As to its influence, this is conditional upon refinement which in turn is dependent upon hearts which are detached and pure. As to its moderation, this hath to be combined with tact and wisdom as prescribed in the Holy Scriptures and Tablets.

Every word is endowed with a spirit, therefore the

speaker or expounder should carefully deliver his words at the appropriate time and place, for the impression which each word maketh is clearly evident and perceptible. The Great Being saith: One word may be likened unto fire, another unto light, and the influence which both exert is manifest in the world. Therefore an enlightened man of wisdom should primarily speak with words as mild as milk, that the children of men may be nurtured and edified thereby and may attain the ultimate goal of human existence which is the station of true understanding and nobility. And likewise He saith: One word is like unto springtime causing the tender saplings of the rose-garden of knowledge to become verdant and flourishing, while another word is even as a deadly poison. It behoveth a prudent man of wisdom to speak with utmost leniency and forbearance so that the sweetness of his words may induce everyone to attain that which befitteth man's station.

O friend of mine! The Word of God is the king of words and its pervasive influence is incalculable. It hath ever dominated and will continue to dominate the realm of being. The Great Being saith: The Word is the master key for the whole world, inasmuch as through its potency the doors of the hearts of men, which in reality are the doors of heaven, are unlocked. No sooner had but a glimmer of its effulgent splendour shone forth upon the mirror of love than the blessed word 'I am the Best-Beloved' was reflected therein. It is an ocean inexhaustible in riches, comprehending all things. Every thing which can be perceived is but an emanation therefrom. High, immeasurably high is this sublime station, in whose shadow moveth the essence of loftiness and splendour, wrapt in praise and adoration.

Methinks people's sense of taste hath, alas, been sorely affected by the fever of negligence and folly, for they are found to be wholly unconscious and deprived of the sweetness of His utterance. How regrettable indeed that man should debar himself from the fruits of the tree of wisdom while his days and hours pass swiftly away. Please God, the hand of divine power may safeguard all mankind and direct their steps towards the horizon of true understanding.

Verily our Lord of Mercy is the Helper, the Knowing, the Wise.

I would like to add that thy second letter which had been sent from Jerusalem hath been received and that which thou hadst written and set forth therein was perused and read in His presence. He bade me write as follows:

O Maqṣúd! We have heard thy voice and perceived the sighing and lamentation thou didst raise in thy longing and eagerness. Praised be God! The sweet savours of love could be inhaled from every word thereof. Please God, this bounty may last for ever. The Servant-in-Attendance recited the verses thou hast composed. Thy name is often mentioned in the presence of this Wronged One and the glances of Our loving-kindness and compassion are directed towards thee.

Great is the station of man. Great must also be his endeavours for the rehabilitation of the world and the well-being of nations. I beseech the One true God to graciously confirm thee in that which beseemeth man's station.

Be thou guided by wisdom under all conditions, inasmuch as persons who harbour evil motives have been and are still diligently engaged in intriguing. Gracious God! Unto that immeasurably exalted Being Who seeketh naught but to foster the spirit of love and fellowship amongst men, and to revive the world and ennoble its life, they have imputed such charges as the tongue and the pen are ashamed to recount.

We have remembered thee and make mention of thee now. We entreat Him—exalted is His glory—to protect thee with the hands of might and power and enable thee to recognize that which will serve thy best interests both in this world and in the next. He is the Lord of Mankind, the Possessor of the Throne on High and of the world below. No God is there besides Him, the Omnipotent, the Powerful. God grant that this Wronged One may observe fidelity. He hath not forgotten nor will He ever forget thee.

Thou hast mentioned thine intention to stay in Damascus until spring, then to proceed to Mosul, should the means be forthcoming. This lowly servant entreateth God—exalted is His glory—to provide such means as is deemed expedient, and to aid thee. He is Potent and Powerful.

Although all the inhabitants of this region have been treated with the utmost kindness, yet no evidence of fellowship can be discerned from them. Thou shouldst observe much tact and wisdom, for they seek at all times to cavil at and deny the Cause. May the One true God grant them equity.

Concerning thine own affairs, if thou wouldst content thyself with whatever might come to pass it would be praiseworthy. To engage in some profession is highly commendable, for when occupied with work one is less likely to dwell on the unpleasant aspects of life. God willing thou mayest experience joy and radiance, gladness and exultation in any city or land where thou mayest happen to sojourn. This lowly servant will never forget that distinguished and kind friend. He hath remembered and will continue to remember thee. The decree lieth with God, the Lord of all worlds. I fain would hope He may vouchsafe divine assistance and grant confirmation in that which is pleasing and acceptable unto Him.

Every word of thy poetry is indeed like unto a mirror in

which the evidences of the devotion and love thou cherishest for God and His chosen ones are reflected. Well is it with thee who hast quaffed the choice wine of utterance and partaken of the soft flowing stream of true knowledge. Happy is he who hath drunk his fill and attained unto Him and woe betide the heedless. Its perusal hath truly proved highly impressive, for it was indicative of both the light of reunion and the fire of separation.

Far be it from us to despair at any time of the incalculable favours of God, for if it were His wish He could cause a mere atom to be transformed into a sun and a single drop into an ocean. He unlocketh thousands of doors, while man is incapable of conceiving even a single one.

So heedless is this servant that with words such as these he seeketh to vindicate the supreme power of God—exalted be His glory. I implore pardon of God, the Most Great, for these assertions and affirm that this servant at all times recognizeth his grievous trespasses and misdeeds. He entreateth remission of his sins from the ocean of the forgiveness of his Lord, the Most Exalted, and beggeth for that which will make him wholly devoted to God and enable him to utter His praise, turn himself toward Him and to put his whole trust in Him. Verily He is the Potent, the Forgiving, the Merciful. Praised be God, the Almighty, the All-Knowing.

This lowly one hath read the descriptions of the dialogue with the traveller which thou hast recounted in thy letter to my Lord, may my life be offered up for His sake. The explanations which were set forth awaken the people from the slumber of heedlessness. Indeed the actions of man himself breed a profusion of satanic power. For were men to abide by and observe the divine teachings, every trace of evil would be banished from the face of the earth. However, the widespread differences that exist among mankind and the prevalence of sedition, contention, conflict and the like are the primary factors which provoke the appearance of the satanic spirit. Yet the Holy Spirit hath ever shunned such matters. A world in which naught can be perceived save strife, quarrels and corruption is bound to become the seat of the throne, the very metropolis, of Satan.

How vast the number of the loved and chosen ones of God who have lamented and moaned by day and by night that haply a sweet and fragrant breeze might blow from the court of His good-pleasure and dispel altogether the loathsome and foul-smelling odours from the world. However, this ultimate goal could not be attained, and men were deprived thereof by virtue of their evil deeds, which brought upon them the retribution of God, in accordance with the basic principles of His divine rule. Ours is the duty to remain patient in these circumstances until relief be forthcoming from God, the Forgiving, the Bountiful.

Magnified be Thy Name, O Lord of all beings and Desire of all created things! I beseech Thee, by the Word which hath caused the Burning Bush to lift up its Voice and the Rock to cry out, whereby the well-favoured have hastened to attain the court of Thy presence and the pure in heart the dayspring of the light of Thy countenance, and by the sighing of Thy true lovers in their separation from Thy chosen ones and by the lamentation of them that long to behold Thy face before the dawning splendour of the light of Thy Revelation, to graciously enable Thy servants to recognize what Thou hast ordained for them by Thy bounty and Thy grace. Prescribe for them then through Thy Pen of Glory that which will direct their steps to the ocean of Thy generosity and will lead them unto the living waters of Thy heavenly reunion.

O Lord! Look not at the things they have wrought, rather look unto the loftiness of Thy celestial bounty which hath preceded all created things, visible and invisible. O Lord! Illumine their hearts with the effulgent light of Thy knowledge and brighten their eyes with the shining splendour of the day-star of Thy favours.

I entreat Thee, O Lord of Names and Creator of the heavens, by the blood spilt in Thy Path, and by the heads carried aloft on spears for the sake of Thy love, and by the souls that have melted in their separation from Thy loved ones, and by the hearts broken for the exaltation of Thy Word, to grant that the dwellers of Thy realm may unite together in their allegiance to Thine incomparable Word so that they may all acknowledge Thy unity and Thy oneness. There is no God but Thee, the Omnipotent, the Most Exalted, the Knowing, the Wise.

I fain would hope that He Who is the All-Sufficing, the Inaccessible, may heed the solicitation of this lowly servant, may attire the people of the world with the raiment of goodly deeds and purge them from evil inclinations. He is the Mighty, the Powerful, the All-Wise, the All-Perceiving. He heareth and seeth; He is the All-Hearing, the All-Seeing.

12

SÚRIY-I-VAFÁ[1]
(Tablet to Vafá)

---

[1] Muḥammad Ḥusayn, one of the early believers of S͟híráz, surnamed 'Vafá' (Fidelity) by Bahá'u'lláh.

VAFÁ! Render thanks unto thy Lord for having aided thee to embrace His Cause, enabled thee to recognize the Manifestation of His Own Self and raised thee up to magnify Him Who is the Most Great Remembrance in this glorious Announcement.

Blessed art thou O Vafá, inasmuch as thou hast been faithful to the Covenant of God and His Testament at a time when all men have violated it and have repudiated the One in Whom they had believed, and this notwithstanding that He hath appeared invested with every testimony, and hath dawned from the horizon of Revelation clothed with undoubted sovereignty.

It behoveth thee, however, to exert thine utmost to attain the very essence of fidelity. This implieth to be well assured in thy heart and to testify with thy tongue to that whereunto God hath testified for His Own exalted Self, proclaiming: 'Verily, self-subsisting am I within the Realm of Glory.' Whoso is enabled in these days to solemnly affirm this truth, hath attained unto all good, and the heavenly Spirit shall descend upon him in the daytime and in the night season, shall graciously assist him to glorify the Name of his Lord and suffer him to unloose his tongue and uphold with his words the Cause of his Lord, the Merciful, the Compassionate. And none can ever achieve this except he who hath purged his heart from whatsoever is created between heaven and earth, and hath entirely detached himself from all but God, the sovereign Lord, the Almighty, the Gracious.

Arise thou to serve the Cause and say: I swear by the righteousness of God! Verily this is the Primal Point, arrayed in His new attire and manifested in His glorious Name. He at present beholdeth everything from this Horizon. Indeed He is supreme over all things. Amongst the Concourse on High He is known as the Most Great Announcement and in the Realms of Eternity as the Ancient Beauty, and before the Throne by this Name[1] which hath caused the footsteps of them that are endued with understanding to slip.

Say, I swear by God! In this Revelation even before a single verse was sent down from the realm of holiness and sublimity, the supreme testimony of God had been fulfilled for all the inmates of heaven and the dwellers on earth; moreover, We have revealed the equivalent of whatsoever was sent down in the Dispensation of the Bayán. Fear ye God and suffer not your deeds to be rendered vain and be not of them that are sunk in heedlessness. Open your eyes that ye may behold the Ancient Beauty from this shining and luminous station.

Say, God is my witness! The Promised One Himself hath come down from heaven, seated upon the crimson cloud with the hosts of revelation on His right, and the angels of inspiration on His left, and the Decree hath been fulfilled at the behest of God, the Omnipotent, the Almighty. Thereupon the footsteps of everyone have slipped except such as God hath protected through His tender mercy and numbered with those who have recog-

[1] The Most Great Name.

nized Him through His Own Self and detached themselves from all that pertaineth to the world.

Hearken thou unto the Words of thy Lord and purify thy heart from every illusion so that the effulgent light of the remembrance of thy Lord may shed its radiance upon it, and it may attain the station of certitude.

Know thou moreover that thy letter reached Our presence and We perceived and perused its contents. We noted the questions thou hast asked and will readily answer thee. It behoveth everyone in this Day to ask God that which he desireth, and thy Lord will heed his petition with wondrous and undeniable verses.

Thou hast asked regarding the subject of the return. Know thou that the end is like unto the beginning. Even as thou dost consider the beginning, similarly shouldst thou consider the end, and be of them that truly perceive. Nay, rather consider the beginning as the end itself, and so conversely, that thou mayest acquire a clear perception. Know thou moreover that every created thing is continually brought forth and returned at the bidding of thy Lord, the God of power and might.

As to the Return, as God hath purposed in His sacred and exalted Tablets wherein He hath made this theme known unto His servants; by this is meant the return of all created things in the Day of Resurrection, and this is indeed the essence of the Return as thou hast witnessed in God's own days and thou art of them that testify to this truth.

Verily God is fully capable of causing all names to appear in one name, and all souls in one soul. Surely powerful and mighty is He. And this Return is realized at His behest in whatever form He willeth. Indeed He is the One Who doeth and ordaineth all things. Moreover, thou shouldst not perceive the fulfilment of the Return and the Resurrection save in the Word of thy Lord, the Almighty, the All-Knowing. For instance, were He to take a handful of earth and declare it to be the One Whom ye have been following in the past, it would undoubtedly be just and true, even as His real Person, and to none is given the right to question His authority. He doeth what He willeth and ordaineth whatsoever He pleaseth. Moreover, in this station take thou heed not to turn thy gaze unto limitations and allusions, but rather unto that whereby the Revelation itself hath been fulfilled and be of them that are discerning. Thus do We explain for thee in a lucid and explicit language that thou mayest comprehend that which thou didst seek from thine ancient Lord.

Consider thou the Day of Resurrection. Were God to pronounce the lowliest of creatures among the faithful to be the First One to believe in the Bayán, thou shouldst have no misgivings about it and must be of them that truly believe. In this station look not upon human limitations and names but rather upon that whereby the rank of the First One to believe is vindicated, which is faith in God, and recognition of His Being and assurance in the fulfilment of His irresistible and binding command.

Consider thou the Revelation of the Point of the Bayán —exalted is His glory. He pronounced the First One[1] to believe in Him to be Muḥammad, the Messenger of God. Doth it beseem a man to dispute with Him by saying that this man is from Persia, the Other from Arabia, or this one was called Ḥusayn while the Other bore the name of Muḥammad? Nay, I swear by God's holy Being, the Exalted, the Most Great. Surely no man of intelligence and insight would ever pay attention unto limitations or names, but rather unto that with which Muḥammad was invested,

[1] Mullá Ḥusayn.

which was none other than the Cause of God. Such a man of insight would likewise consider Ḥusayn and the position he occupied in the Cause of God, the Omnipotent, the Exalted, the Knowing, the Wise. And since the First One to believe in God in the Dispensation of the Bayán was invested with command similar to that with which Muḥammad, the Messenger of God, was invested, therefore the Báb pronounced him to be the latter, namely His return and resurrection. This station is sanctified from every limitation or name, and naught can be seen therein but God, the One, the Peerless, the All-Knowing.

Know thou moreover that in the Day of Revelation were He to pronounce one of the leaves to be the manifestation of all His excellent titles, unto no one is given the right to utter why or wherefore, and should one do so he would be regarded as a disbeliever in God and be numbered with such as have repudiated His Truth.

Beware, beware lest thou behave like unto the people of the Bayán. For indeed they erred grievously, misguided the people, ignored the Covenant of God and His Testament and joined partners with Him, the One, the Incomparable, the All-Knowing. Verily they failed to recognize the Point of the Bayán, for had they recognized Him they would not have rejected His manifestation in this luminous and resplendent Being. And since they fixed their eyes on names, therefore when He replaced His Name 'the Most Exalted' by 'the Most Glorious' their eyes were dimmed. They have failed to recognize Him in these days and are reckoned with those that perish. Indeed, had they known Him through His own Self or by virtue of that which He hath revealed, they would not have repudiated Him when He appeared in this glorious and incomparable Name, which God hath ordained to be the Sword of His Revelation between heaven and earth, and through which truth is separated from error, even from now until the Day when mankind shall stand before the Lord of the worlds.

Know thou moreover that in the Day of His Manifestation all things besides God shall be brought forth and placed equally, irrespective of their rank being high or low. The Day of Return is inscrutable unto all men until after the divine Revelation hath been fulfilled. He is in truth the One Who ordaineth whatsoever He willeth. When the Word of God is revealed unto all created things whoso then giveth ear and heedeth the Call is, indeed, reckoned among the most distinguished souls, though he be a carrier of ashes. And he who turneth away is accounted as the lowliest of His servants, though he be a ruler amongst men and the possessor of all the books that are in the heavens and on earth.

It behoveth thee to look with divine insight upon the things We have revealed and sent unto thee and not towards the people and that which is current amongst them. They are in this day like unto a blind man who, while moving in the sunshine, demandeth: Where is the sun? Is it shining? He would deny and dispute the truth, and would not be of them that perceive. Never shall he be able to discern the sun or to understand that which hath intervened between him and it. He would object within himself, voice protests, and would be among the rebellious. Such is the state of this people. Leave them unto themselves, saying: Unto you be that which ye desire and unto us that which we desire. Wretched indeed is the plight of the ungodly.

Know thou moreover that the former Manifestation affirmed that the return and rising of the spirits would occur on the Day of Resurrection, while in truth there is a return and resurrection for every created thing. However We do not wish to mention aught that is not set forth in the Bayán, lest perchance the people of malice raise a great outcry. O would that that which interveneth between the children of men and their Creator were dispelled that they might be enabled to behold God's invincible sovereignty and dominion, quaff from the wellspring of His heavenly streams, be sprinkled with the outpourings of the ocean of true understanding and be purged from the defilements of the ungodly and the suspicious.

As to thy question concerning the worlds of God. Know thou of a truth that the worlds of God are countless in their number, and infinite in their range. None can reckon or comprehend them except God, the All-Knowing, the All-Wise. Consider thy state when asleep. Verily, I say, this phenomenon is the most mysterious of the signs of God amongst men, were they to ponder it in their hearts. Behold how the thing which thou hast seen in thy dream is, after a considerable lapse of time, fully realized. Had the world in which thou didst find thyself in thy dream been identical with the world in which thou livest, it would have been necessary for the event occurring in that dream to have transpired in this world at the very moment of its occurrence. Were it so, you yourself would have borne witness unto it. This being not the case, however, it must necessarily follow that the world in which thou livest is different and apart from that which thou hast experienced in thy dream. This latter world hath neither beginning nor end. It would be true if thou wert to contend that this same world is, as decreed by the All-Glorious and Almighty God, within thy proper self and is wrapped up within thee. It would equally be true to maintain that thy spirit, having transcended the limitations of sleep and having stripped itself of all earthly attachment, hath, by the act of God, been made to traverse a realm which lieth hidden in the innermost reality of this world. Verily I say, the creation of God embraceth worlds besides this world, and creatures apart from these creatures. In each of these worlds He hath ordained things which none can search except Himself, the All-Searching, the All-Wise. Do thou meditate on that which We have revealed unto thee, that thou mayest discover the purpose of God, thy Lord, and the Lord of all worlds. In these words the mysteries of Divine Wisdom have been treasured. We have refrained from dwelling upon this theme owing to the sorrow that hath encompassed Us from the actions of them that have been created through Our words, if ye be of them that will hearken unto Our Voice.

Where is the one who can help Me and shield Me from the swords of these faithless souls? Where is the man of insight who will behold the Words of God with his own eyes and rid himself of the opinions and notions of the peoples of the earth?

O servant! Warn thou the servants of God not to reject that which they do not comprehend. Say, implore God to open to your hearts the portals of true understanding that ye may be apprised of that of which no one is apprised. Verily, He is the Giver, the Forgiving, the Compassionate.

Thou hast moreover asked Me concerning the ordinances of God. Know thou of a truth that whatsoever hath been prescribed in the Book is indeed the truth, no doubt is there about it, and it is incumbent upon everyone to observe that which hath been sent down by Him Who is the Revealer, the All-Knowing. Were a man to put them away despite his being aware thereof, God would truly be clear of such a one and We too would be clear of him, inasmuch as His ordinances constitute the fruits of the divine Tree and none other than the heedless and the wayward will deviate therefrom.

As to Paradise: It is a reality and there can be no doubt about it, and now in this world it is realized through love of Me and My good-pleasure. Whosoever attaineth unto it God will aid him in this world below, and after death He will enable him to gain admittance into Paradise whose vastness is as that of heaven and earth. Therein the Maids of glory and holiness will wait upon him in the daytime and in the night season, while the day-star of the unfading beauty of his Lord will at all times shed its radiance upon him and he will shine so brightly that no one shall bear to gaze at him. Such is the dispensation of Providence, yet the people are shut out by a grievous veil. Likewise apprehend thou the nature of hell-fire and be of them that truly believe. For every act performed there shall be a recompense according to the estimate of God, and unto this the very ordinances and prohibitions prescribed by the Almighty amply bear witness. For surely if deeds were not rewarded and yielded no fruit, then the Cause of God —exalted is He—would prove futile. Immeasurably high is He exalted above such blasphemies! However, unto them that are rid of all attachments a deed is, verily, its own reward. Were We to enlarge upon this theme numerous Tablets would need to be written.

I swear by the righteousness of the One true God! The Pen is unable to move by reason of that which hath befallen its Lord, and it weepeth sore, and so do I weep, and likewise weepeth the eye of Him Who is the Essence of Grandeur behind the Tabernacle of Names while seated on the Throne of His glorious Name.

Purge thou thy heart that We may cause fountains of

wisdom and utterance to gush out therefrom, thus enabling thee to raise thy voice among all mankind. Unloose thy tongue and proclaim the truth for the sake of the remembrance of thy merciful Lord. Be not afraid of anyone, place thy whole trust in God, the Almighty, the All-Knowing. Say, O people, fulfil whatever ye understand of the Persian Bayán and whatever ye understand not ask this unerring Remembrance that He may set forth clearly that which God hath intended in His Book, for in truth He knoweth that which is enshrined in the Bayán by virtue of the Will of Him Who is the Omnipotent, the Powerful.

Thou hast enquired about the warning We gave to the people at the time of Our departure from 'Iráq to the effect that when the Sun disappeareth from sight, birds of darkness will be in motion and the standards of Sámirí[1] will be reared high. I swear by God! Those birds have stirred in these days and Sámirí hath raised his clamour. Well is it with him who recognizeth and is numbered with men of understanding. We have also warned them against the appearance of the calf. God is My witness! All Our warnings have come to pass, as indeed, they are bound to, inasmuch as they have issued from the fingers of glory and might. Beseech thou God to protect thee from the mischief of these men and to purify thee from the insinuations of the froward. Strengthen thy loins then for the promotion of the Cause and pay no attention unto the words uttered by the people of the Bayán, for they are truly incapable of understanding and have failed to comprehend the essence of the Cause as is revealed in this august, this Most Great Announcement. Thus have We inspired thee, and infused into thy heart that which will make thee independent of the allusions of mankind.

[1] The maker of the Golden Calf. See Qur'án 20:87-98.

The glory of God be upon thee and upon them that give ear unto the words thou dost utter for the love of God, thy Lord, and remain steadfast in His Cause. All praise be unto God, the Lord of the worlds.

13

LAWḤ-I-SIYYID-I-MIHDÍY-I-DAHAJÍ

(Tablet to Siyyid Mihdíy-i-Dahají)

He is the Most Holy, the Most Great, the Most Exalted,
the Most High

O MY Name![1] Yield thou praise unto God for having graciously chosen thee to be a shower of bounty for that which We have sown in the pure and blessed soil and enabled thee to serve as a springtime of tender mercy for the wondrous and sublime trees We have planted. Indeed so great is this favour that of all created things in the world of existence, none can ever hope to rival it. We have moreover given thee to drink the choice wine of utterance from the chalice of the heavenly bestowals of thy merciful Lord, which is none other than this Tongue of holiness—a Tongue that, as soon as it was unloosed, quickened the entire creation, set in motion all beings and caused the Nightingale to pour forth its melodies. This is the Fountain of living water for all that dwell in the realm of being.

Oftentimes have We wafted upon thee the sweet savours of the All-Merciful from this Branch which moveth over the Tablet of thy Lord, the Mighty, the Unconstrained. By the righteousness of the One true God! Were all created things, visible and invisible, to direct themselves towards

[1] Siyyid Mihdíy-i-Dahají, to whom this Tablet was addressed, had been given by Bahá'u'lláh the title Ismu'lláhi'l-Mihdí, 'The Name of God, Mihdí'. He later broke the Covenant. (See *God Passes By*, page 319.)

Him, thou wouldst find them winging their flight unto the Supreme Goal, the Spot wherein the divine Lote-Tree exclaimeth: Verily, no God is there but Me, the Almighty, the All-Bountiful.

Great is thy blessedness, inasmuch as thou hast been journeying throughout the lands of God, and been the embodiment of joy and assurance for the people of Bahá who have renounced all else but Him, and set their hearts towards this Court which hath shed its radiance upon all realms, and sprinkled them with the surging waters of this Ocean wherewith thou thyself hast been sprinkled—an Ocean which hath encompassed all created things.

Indeed thou didst grasp the significance of rendering assistance unto God and didst arise to achieve this through the power of wisdom and utterance. Say: To assist Me is to teach My Cause. This is a theme with which whole Tablets are laden. This is the changeless commandment of God, eternal in the past, eternal in the future. Comprehend this, O ye men of insight. They that have passed beyond the bounds of wisdom fail to understand the meaning of assisting God as set forth in the Book. Say: Fear ye God and sow not the seeds of dissension amongst men. Observe ye that which hath been enjoined upon you by your Lord, the Almighty, the All-Knowing. He knoweth the reality of victory and hath taught it to you with an utterance that the vain imaginings of them that rove distraught in the wilderness of doubt can never corrupt.

O My Name! Suffer all created things to quaff once again from this chalice which hath caused the seas to rise. Kindle then in the hearts the blazing fire which this crimson Tree hath ignited, that they may arise to extol and magnify His Name amidst the adherents of all Faiths.

Numerous letters from thee have been presented before

Our Throne. We have perused them as a token of grace on Our part, and for each name thou didst mention therein We have revealed that which will stir the minds of men and will cause the spirits to soar. Moreover We have repeatedly enabled thee to hearken unto the warblings of the birds of heaven and to incline thine ear to the songs of the nightingales pouring forth their melodies upon the branches. Thus was the Pen of God set in motion in thy remembrance that thou mightest admonish men through the power of this utterance which is divinely ordained to be the revealer of the signs of His glory.

Blessed is the spot wherein the anthem of His praise is raised, and blessed the ear that hearkeneth unto that which hath been sent down from the heaven of the loving-kindness of thy Lord, the All-Merciful.

Exhort thou the servants of God unto that whereunto We have exhorted thee that they may abstain from whatsoever is forbidden them in the Mother Book. Those who perpetrate deeds that would create turmoil among the people have indeed strayed far from helping God and His Cause and are numbered with the mischief-makers in the Tablet which God hath designated to be the dawning-place of all Tablets.

Say: If it be Our pleasure We shall render the Cause victorious through the power of a single word from Our presence. He is in truth the Omnipotent, the All-Compelling. Should it be God's intention, there would appear out of the forests of celestial might the lion of indomitable strength whose roaring is like unto the peals of thunder reverberating in the mountains. However, since Our loving providence surpasseth all things, We have ordained that complete victory should be achieved through speech and utterance, that Our servants throughout the earth may thereby become the recipients of divine good. This is but a token of God's bounty vouchsafed unto them. Verily thy Lord is the All-Sufficing, the Most Exalted.

Say: Fear ye God and commit not such deeds as would cause My loved ones on earth to lament. Thus biddeth you this Pen which hath set the Pen of Glory in motion within the arena of wisdom and true understanding.

Convey My greetings unto those whose faces mirror forth the radiance of Bahá, then mention to them this utterance which cheereth the eyes of the righteous. The glory of God rest upon thee and upon such as have firmly clung to the Cord of God, the Revealer of verses. . . .

Restrain thou the inhabitants of those regions from provocative acts, from strife, dissension or aught else that would create trouble. That which is praiseworthy in these days is the promotion of the Cause. For instance if those people who pursue certain aims were to dedicate themselves to the teaching of the Cause, all the dwellers of those regions would, ere long, be invested with the mantle of faith.

Should anyone perceive the sweetness of the following passage in the Tablet revealed in honour of Nabíl of Qá'in,[1] he would readily comprehend the significance of assistance: Human utterance is an essence which aspireth to exert its influence and needeth moderation. As to its influence, this is conditional upon refinement, which in turn is dependent upon hearts which are detached and pure. As to its moderation, this hath to be combined with tact and wisdom as prescribed in the Holy Scriptures and Tablets.

O My Name! Utterance must needs possess penetrating power. For if bereft of this quality it would fail to exert

[1] Nabíl-i-Akbar. See p. 135.

influence. And this penetrating influence dependeth on the spirit being pure and the heart stainless. Likewise it needeth moderation, without which the hearer would be unable to bear it, rather he would manifest opposition from the very outset. And moderation will be obtained by blending utterance with the tokens of divine wisdom which are recorded in the sacred Books and Tablets. Thus when the essence of one's utterance is endowed with these two requisites it will prove highly effective and will be the prime factor in transforming the souls of men. This is the station of supreme victory and celestial dominion. Whoso attaineth thereto is invested with the power to teach the Cause of God and to prevail over the hearts and minds of men.

O My Name! The Day-Star of utterance, shining resplendent from the dayspring of divine Revelation, hath so illumined the Scrolls and Tablets that the kingdom of utterance and the exalted dominion of understanding vibrate with joy and ecstasy and shine forth with the splendour of His light, yet the generality of mankind comprehend not.

The reason why the subject of aid and assistance hath time and again streamed and will continue to stream from the Pen of Providence is to warn the friends of God lest they engage in activities that would give rise to strife and turmoil. It is incumbent upon them, one and all, to diligently seek ways to help the Cause of God in such manner as We have explained. This is but a token of His grace especially conferred upon His loved ones that every one of them may attain the station characterized by the words: 'Whoso quickeneth a soul hath verily quickened all mankind.'

Temporal ascendancy hath been and will continue to be under the shadow of this station. Its appointed hour is preordained in the Book of God. He is truly cognizant thereof and it will be manifested through the potency of His might. Verily He is the Powerful, the All-Subduing, the Omnipotent, the All-Knowing, the All-Wise.

The sanctified souls should ponder and meditate in their hearts regarding the methods of teaching. From the texts of the wondrous, heavenly Scriptures they should memorize phrases and passages bearing on various instances, so that in the course of their speech they may recite divine verses whenever the occasion demandeth it, inasmuch as these holy verses are the most potent elixir, the greatest and mightiest talisman. So potent is their influence that the hearer will have no cause for vacillation. I swear by My life! This Revelation is endowed with such a power that it will act as the lodestone for all nations and kindreds of the earth. Should one pause to meditate attentively he would recognize that no place is there, nor can there be, for anyone to flee to.

In such manner hath the *Kitáb-i-Aqdas* been revealed that it attracteth and embraceth all the divinely appointed Dispensations. Blessed those who peruse it. Blessed those who apprehend it. Blessed those who meditate upon it. Blessed those who ponder its meaning. So vast is its range that it hath encompassed all men ere their recognition of it. Ere long will its sovereign power, its pervasive influence and the greatness of its might be manifested on earth. Verily, thy God is the All-Knowing, the All-Informed.

O My Name! Hearken thou unto My Voice coming from the direction of My Throne. He wisheth to make mention of thy name at all times inasmuch as thou hast proved thyself steadfast in extolling His virtues amongst men. Indeed thy Lord loveth fidelity as found in the realm of creation, and He hath given it precedence over most of the praiseworthy qualities. Verily, He is Potent and Powerful.

Know thou moreover that We have heard the praise thou hast uttered in thy communion with God, thy Lord, the Exalted, the Gracious. Great indeed is the blessedness awaiting thee, inasmuch as thou hast curtailed thine own affairs in favour of this inviolable, this mighty and enlightened Cause. We entreat God to make thy call a magnet which will attract the embodiments of names in the world of existence that all beings may spontaneously hasten to heed it. No God is there besides Him, the Exalted, the Pre-Eminent, the Ever-Blessed, the Sublime, the Most August, the Most Glorious, the Most Bountiful, the All-Knowing, the All-Informed.

14

LAWḤ-I-BURHÁN

(Tablet of the Proof)

This Tablet was revealed after the martyrdom of the King of Martyrs and the Beloved of Martyrs (see God Passes By pages 200–201) and was addressed to Shaykh Muḥammad Báqir, denounced by Bahá'u'lláh as the 'Wolf'. In this Tablet Bahá'u'lláh refers to Mír Muḥammad Ḥusayn, the Imám Jum'ih of Iṣfahán, surnamed the 'She-Serpent', who was Shaykh Muḥammad Báqir's accomplice in the persecution of the Bahá'ís. (See God Passes By, pages 198, 200–201 and 219). The Epistle to the Son of the Wolf was addressed to Shaykh Muḥammad Taqíy-i-Najafí, the son of Shaykh Muḥammad Báqir.

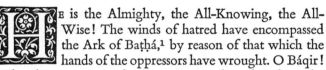ᴇ is the Almighty, the All-Knowing, the All-Wise! The winds of hatred have encompassed the Ark of Baṭḥá,[1] by reason of that which the hands of the oppressors have wrought. O Báqir! Thou hast pronounced sentence against them for whom the books of the world have wept, and in whose favour the scriptures of all religions have testified. Thou, who art gone far astray, art indeed wrapt in a thick veil. By God Himself! Thou hast pronounced judgement against them through whom the horizon of faith hath been illumined. Unto this bear witness They Who are the Dawning-Places of Revelation and the Manifestations of the Cause of thy Lord, the Most Merciful, Who have sacrificed Their souls and all that They possessed in His straight Path. The Faith of God hath cried everywhere, by reason of thy tyranny, and yet thou disportest thyself and art of them that exult. There is no hatred in Mine heart for thee nor for anyone. Every man of learning beholdeth thee, and such as are like thee, engulfed in evident folly. Hadst thou realized that which thou hast done, thou wouldst have cast thyself into the fire, or abandoned thine home and fled into the mountains, or wouldst have groaned until thou hadst returned unto the place destined for thee by Him Who is the Lord of strength and of might. O thou who art even as nothing! Rend thou asunder the veils of idle fancies and vain imaginings, that thou mayest behold the Day-Star of knowledge shining

---

[1] Mecca.

from this resplendent Horizon. Thou hast torn in pieces a remnant of the Prophet Himself, and imagined that thou hadst helped the Faith of God. Thus hath thy soul prompted thee, and thou art truly one of the heedless. Thine act hath consumed the hearts of the Concourse on high, and those of such as have circled round the Cause of God, the Lord of the worlds. The soul of the Chaste One[1] melted, by reason of thy cruelty, and the inmates of Paradise wept sore in that blessed Spot.

Judge thou fairly, I adjure thee by God. What proof did the Jewish doctors adduce wherewith to condemn Him Who was the Spirit of God,[2] when He came unto them with truth? What could have been the evidence produced by the Pharisees and the idolatrous priests to justify their denial of Muḥammad, the Apostle of God when He came unto them with a Book that judged between truth and falsehood with a justice which turned into light the darkness of the earth, and enraptured the hearts of such as had known Him? Indeed thou hast produced, in this day, the same proofs which the foolish divines advanced in that age. Unto this testifieth He Who is the King of the realm of grace in this great Prison. Thou hast, truly, walked in their ways, nay, hast surpassed them in their cruelty, and hast deemed thyself to be helping the Faith and defending the Law of God, the All-Knowing, the All-Wise. By Him Who is the Truth! Thine iniquity hath made Gabriel to groan, and hath drawn tears from the Law of God, through which the breezes of justice have been wafted over all who are in heaven and on earth. Hast thou fondly imagined that the judgement thou didst pronounce hath profited thee? Nay, by Him Who is the King of all Names! Unto thy loss

[1] Fáṭimih, daughter of Muḥammad.
[2] Jesus.

testifieth He with Whom is the knowledge of all things as recorded in the preserved Tablet. When thou didst pen thy judgement, thou wast accused by thy very pen. Unto this doth bear witness the Pen of God, the Most High, in His inaccessible station.

O thou who hast gone astray! Thou hast neither seen Me, nor associated with Me, nor been My companion for the fraction of a moment. How is it, then, that thou hast bidden men to curse Me? Didst thou, in this, follow the promptings of thine own desires, or didst thou obey thy Lord? Produce thou a sign, if thou art one of the truthful. We testify that thou hast cast behind thy back the Law of God, and laid hold on the dictates of thy passions. Nothing, in truth, escapeth His knowledge; He, verily, is the Incomparable, the All-Informed. O heedless one! Hearken unto that which the Merciful hath revealed in the Qur'án: 'Say not to every one who meeteth you with a greeting, "Thou art not a believer."'[1] Thus hath He decreed in Whose grasp are the kingdoms of Revelation and of creation, if thou be of them that hearken. Thou hast set aside the commandment of God, and clung unto the promptings of thine own desire. Woe, then, unto thee, O careless one that doubtest! If thou deniest Me, by what proof canst thou vindicate the truth of that which thou dost possess? Produce it, then, O thou who hast joined partners with God, and turned aside from His sovereignty that hath encompassed the worlds!

O foolish one! Know thou that he is truly learned who hath acknowledged My Revelation, and drunk from the Ocean of My knowledge, and soared in the atmosphere of My love, and cast away all else besides Me, and taken firm hold on that which hath been sent down from the Kingdom

[1] Qur'án 4:96.

of My wondrous utterance. He, verily, is even as an eye unto mankind, and as the spirit of life unto the body of all creation. Glorified be the All-Merciful Who hath enlightened him, and caused him to arise and serve His great and mighty Cause. Verily, such a man is blessed by the Concourse on high, and by them who dwell within the Tabernacle of Grandeur, who have quaffed My sealed Wine in My Name, the Omnipotent, the All-Powerful. O Báqir! If thou be of them that occupy such a sublime station, produce then a sign from God, the Creator of the heavens. And shouldst thou recognize thy powerlessness, do thou rein in thy passions, and return unto thy Lord, that perchance He may forgive thee thy sins which have caused the leaves of the Divine Lote-Tree to be burnt up, and the Rock to cry out, and the eyes of men of understanding to weep. Because of thee the Veil of Divinity was rent asunder, and the Ark foundered, and the She-Camel was hamstrung, and the Spirit[1] groaned in His sublime retreat. Disputest thou with Him Who hath come unto thee with the testimonies of God and His signs which thou possessest and which are in the possession of them that dwell on earth? Open thine eyes that thou mayest behold this Wronged One shining forth above the horizon of the will of God, the Sovereign, the Truth, the Resplendent. Unstop, then, the ear of thine heart that thou mayest hearken unto the speech of the Divine Lote-Tree that hath been raised up in truth by God, the Almighty, the Beneficent. Verily, this Tree, notwithstanding the things that befell it by reason of thy cruelty and of the transgressions of such as are like thee, calleth aloud and summoneth all men unto the Sadratu'l-Muntahá[2] and the Supreme Horizon. Blessed

---

[1] Jesus.

[2] The Sacred Lote-Tree, the Tree beyond which there is no

is the soul that hath gazed on the Most Mighty Sign, and the ear that hath heard His most sweet Voice, and woe to whosoever hath turned aside and done wickedly.

O thou who hast turned away from God! Wert thou to look with the eye of fairness upon the Divine Lote-Tree, thou wouldst perceive the marks of thy sword on its boughs, and its branches, and its leaves, notwithstanding that God created thee for the purpose of recognizing and of serving it. Reflect, that haply thou mayest recognize thine iniquity and be numbered with such as have repented. Thinkest thou that We fear thy cruelty? Know thou and be well assured that from the first day whereon the voice of the Most Sublime Pen was raised betwixt earth and heaven We offered up Our souls, and Our bodies, and Our sons, and Our possessions in the path of God, the Exalted, the Great, and We glory therein amongst all created things and the Concourse on high. Unto this testify the things which have befallen Us in this straight Path. By God! Our hearts were consumed, and Our bodies were crucified, and Our blood was spilt, while Our eyes were fixed on the horizon of the loving-kindness of their Lord, the Witness, the All-Seeing. The more grievous their woes, the greater waxed the love of the people of Bahá. Unto their sincerity hath borne witness what the All-Merciful hath sent down in the Qur'án. He saith: 'Wish ye, then, for death, if ye are sincere.'[1] Who is to be preferred, he that hath sheltered himself behind curtains, or he that hath offered himself in the path of God? Judge thou fairly, and be not of them that rove distraught in the wilderness of falsehood. So carried

passing (see Qur'án 53:8–18). A symbol of the Manifestation of God. (See *God Passes By* p. 94.)

[1] Qur'án 2:88.

away have they been by the living waters of the love of the Most Merciful, that neither the arms of the world nor the swords of the nations have deterred them from setting their faces towards the ocean of the bounty of their Lord, the Giver, the Generous.

By God! Troubles have failed to unnerve Me, and the repudiation of the divines hath been powerless to weaken Me. I have spoken, and still speak forth before the face of men: 'The door of grace hath been unlocked and He Who is the Dayspring of Justice is come with perspicuous signs and evident testimonies, from God, the Lord of strength and of might!' Present thyself before Me that thou mayest hear the mysteries which were heard by the Son of 'Imrán[1] upon the Sinai of Wisdom. Thus commandeth thee He Who is the Dawning-Place of the Revelation of thy Lord, the God of Mercy, from His great Prison.

Hath leadership made thee proud? Peruse thou what God hath revealed to the Sovereign ruler, the Sultán of Turkey, who hath incarcerated Me in this fortified stronghold, so that thou mayest be informed of the condition of this Wronged One, as decreed by God, the One, the Single, the All-Informed. Art thou happy to see the abject and worthless as thy followers? They support thee as did a people before them, they that followed Annas, who, without clear proof and testimony, pronounced judgement against the Spirit.[2]

Peruse thou the *Kitáb-i-Íqán* and that which the All-Merciful hath sent down unto the King of Paris[3] and to such as are like him, that thou mayest be made aware of the things that have happened in the past, and be persuaded

[1] Moses.
[2] Jesus.
[3] Napoleon III.

that We have not sought to spread disorder in the land
after it had been well-ordered. We exhort, wholly for the
sake of God, His servants. Let him who wisheth turn unto
Him, and him who wisheth turn aside. Our Lord, the
Merciful, is verily the All-Sufficing, the All-Praised. O
concourse of divines! This is the day whereon nothing
amongst all things, nor any name amongst all names, can
profit you save through this Name which God hath made
the Manifestation of His Cause and the Dayspring of His
Most Excellent Titles unto all who are in the kingdom of
creation. Blessed is that man that hath recognized the
fragrance of the All-Merciful and been numbered with the
steadfast. Your sciences shall not profit you in this day, nor
your arts, nor your treasures, nor your glory. Cast them all
behind your backs, and set your faces towards the Most
Sublime Word through which the Scriptures and the
Books and this lucid Tablet have been distinctly set forth.
Cast away, O concourse of divines, the things ye have
composed with the pens of your idle fancies and vain
imaginings. By God! The Day-Star of Knowledge hath
shone forth above the horizon of certitude.

O Báqir! Read and call thou to mind that which was
said of old by a believer of thy stock: 'Will ye slay a man
because he saith my Lord is God, when He hath already
come to you with signs from your Lord? If he be a liar, on
him will be his lie, but if he be a man of truth, part of what
he threateneth will fall upon you. In truth God guideth not
him who is a transgressor, a liar.'[1]

O thou who art gone astray! If thou hast any doubt
concerning Our conduct, know thou that We bear witness
unto that whereunto God hath Himself borne witness ere
the creation of the heavens and of the earth, that there is

1 Qur'án 40:29.

none other God but Him, the Almighty, the All-Bounteous. We testify that He is One in His Essence, One in His attributes. He hath none to equal Him in the whole universe, nor any partner in all creation. He hath sent forth His Messengers, and sent down His Books, that they may announce unto His creatures the Straight Path.

Hath the Sháh been informed, and chosen to close his eyes to thine acts? Or hath he been seized with fear at the howling of a pack of wolves who have cast the Path of God behind their backs and followed in thy way without any clear proof or Book? We have heard that the provinces of Persia have been adorned with the adornment of justice. When We observed closely, however, We found them to be the dawning-places of tyranny and the daysprings of injustice. We behold justice in the clutches of tyranny. We beseech God to set it free through the power of His might and His sovereignty. He, verily, overshadoweth all that is in the heavens and on earth. To none is given the right to protest against anyone concerning that which hath befallen the Cause of God. It behoveth whosoever hath set his face towards the Most Sublime Horizon to cleave tenaciously unto the cord of patience, and to put his reliance in God, the Help in Peril, the Unconstrained. O ye loved ones of God! Drink your fill from the well-spring of wisdom, and walk ye in the garden of wisdom, and soar ye in the atmosphere of wisdom, and speak forth with wisdom and eloquence. Thus biddeth you your Lord, the Almighty, the All-Knowing.

O Báqir! Rely not on thy glory, and thy power. Thou art even as the last trace of sunlight upon the mountain-top. Soon will it fade away, as decreed by God, the All-Possessing, the Most High. Thy glory and the glory of such as are like thee have been taken away, and this verily is

what hath been ordained by the One with Whom is the
Mother Tablet. Where is he to be found who contended
with God, and whither is gone he that gainsaid His signs,
and turned aside from His sovereignty? Where are they
who have slain His chosen ones and spilt the blood of His
holy ones? Reflect, that haply thou mayest perceive the
breaths of thine acts, O foolish doubter! Because of you
the Apostle[1] lamented, and the Chaste One[2] cried out, and
the countries were laid waste, and darkness fell upon all
regions. O concourse of divines! Because of you the people
were abased, and the banner of Islám was hauled down,
and its mighty throne subverted. Every time a man of
discernment hath sought to hold fast unto that which
would exalt Islám, ye raised a clamour, and thereby was he
deterred from achieving his purpose, while the land remained fallen in clear ruin.

Consider the Sulṭán of Turkey! He did not want war,
but those like you desired it. When its fires were enkindled
and its flames rose high, the government and the people
were thereby weakened. Unto this beareth witness every
man of equity and perception. Its calamities waxed so great
that the smoke thereof surrounded the Land of Mystery[3]
and its environs, and what had been revealed in the Tablet
of the Sulṭán was made manifest. Thus hath it been decreed
in the Book, at the behest of God, the Help in Peril, the
Self-Subsisting.

O My Supreme Pen! Leave Thou the mention of the
Wolf, and call Thou to remembrance the She-Serpent[4]
whose cruelty hath caused all created things to groan, and

[1] Muḥammad.

[2] Fáṭimih, daughter of Muḥammad.

[3] Adrianople.

[4] The Imám-Jum'ih of Iṣfahán, see page 203.

the limbs of the holy ones to quake. Thus biddeth Thee the Lord of all names, in this glorious station. The Chaste One[1] hath cried out by reason of thine iniquity, and yet thou dost imagine thyself to be of the family of the Apostle of God! Thus hath thy soul prompted thee, O thou who hast withdrawn thyself from God, the Lord of all that hath been and shall be. Judge thou equitably, O She-Serpent! For what crime didst thou sting the children[2] of the Apostle of God, and pillage their possessions? Hast thou denied Him Who created thee by His command 'be, and it was'? Thou hast dealt with the children of the Apostle of God as neither 'Ád hath dealt with Húd, nor Thamúd with Ṣáliḥ, nor the Jews with the Spirit of God,[3] the Lord of all being. Gainsayest thou the signs of thy Lord which no sooner were sent down from the heaven of His Cause than all the books of the world bowed down before them? Meditate, that thou mayest be made aware of thine act, O heedless outcast! Ere long will the breaths of chastisement seize thee, as they seized others before thee. Wait, O thou who hast joined partners with God, the Lord of the visible and the invisible. This is the day which God hath announced through the tongue of His Apostle. Reflect, that thou mayest apprehend what the All-Merciful hath sent down in the Qur'án and in this inscribed Tablet. This is the day whereon He Who is the Dayspring of Revelation hath come with clear tokens which none can number. This is the day whereon every man endued with perception hath discovered the fragrance of the breeze of the All-Merciful in the world of creation, and every man of insight hath hastened unto the living waters of the mercy of His Lord,

---

[1] Fáṭimih.

[2] The King of Martyrs and the Beloved of Martyrs.

[3] Jesus.

the King of Kings. O heedless one! The tale of the Sacrifice[1] hath been retold, and he who was to be offered up hath directed his steps towards the place of sacrifice, and returned not, by reason of that which thy hand hath wrought, O perverse hater! Didst thou imagine that martyrdom could abase this Cause? Nay, by Him Whom God hath made to be the Repository of His Revelation, if thou be of them that comprehend. Woe betide thee, O thou who hast joined partners with God, and woe betide them that have taken thee as their leader, without a clear token or a perspicuous Book. How numerous the oppressors before thee who have arisen to quench the light of God, and how many the impious who murdered and pillaged until the hearts and souls of men groaned by reason of their cruelty! The sun of justice hath been obscured, inasmuch as the embodiment of tyranny hath been stablished upon the throne of hatred, and yet the people understand not. The children of the Apostle have been slain and their possessions pillaged. Say: Was it, in thine estimation, their possessions or themselves that denied God? Judge fairly, O ignorant one that hath been shut out as by a veil from God. Thou hast clung to tyranny and cast away justice; whereupon all created things have lamented, and still thou art among the wayward. Thou hast put to death the aged, and plundered the young. Thinkest thou that thou wilt consume that which thine iniquity hath amassed? Nay, by Myself! Thus informeth thee He Who is cognizant of all. By God! The things thou possessest shall profit thee not, nor what thou hast laid up through thy cruelty. Unto this beareth witness Thy Lord, the All-Knowing. Thou hast arisen to put out the light of this Cause; ere long will thine own fire be quenched, at His behest. He, verily, is the Lord

[1] Ishmael.

of strength and of might. The changes and chances of the world, and the powers of the nations, cannot frustrate Him. He doeth what He pleaseth, and ordaineth what He willeth through the power of His sovereignty. Consider the she-camel. Though but a beast, yet hath the All-Merciful exalted her to so high a station that the tongues of the earth made mention of her and celebrated her praise. He, verily, overshadoweth all that is in the heavens and on earth. No God is there but Him, the Almighty, the Great. Thus have We adorned the heaven of Our Tablet with the suns of Our words. Blessed the man that hath attained thereunto and been illumined with their light, and woe betide such as have turned aside, and denied Him, and strayed far from Him. Praised be God, the Lord of the worlds!

15

KITÁB-I-'AHD

(Book of the Covenant)

LTHOUGH the Realm of Glory hath none of the vanities of the world, yet within the treasury of trust and resignation We have bequeathed to Our heirs an excellent and priceless heritage. Earthly treasures We have not bequeathed, nor have We added such cares as they entail. By God! In earthly riches fear is hidden and peril is concealed. Consider ye and call to mind that which the All-Merciful hath revealed in the Qur'án: 'Woe betide every slanderer and defamer, him that layeth up riches and counteth them.'[1] Fleeting are the riches of the world; all that perisheth and changeth is not, and hath never been, worthy of attention, except to a recognized measure.

The aim of this Wronged One in sustaining woes and tribulations, in revealing the Holy Verses and in demonstrating proofs hath been naught but to quench the flame of hate and enmity, that the horizon of the hearts of men may be illumined with the light of concord and attain real peace and tranquillity. From the dawning-place of the divine Tablet the day-star of this utterance shineth resplendent, and it behoveth everyone to fix his gaze upon it: We exhort you, O peoples of the world, to observe that which will elevate your station. Hold fast to the fear of God and firmly adhere to what is right. Verily I say, the tongue is for mentioning what is good, defile it not with unseemly talk. God hath forgiven what is past. Henceforward everyone

[1] Qur'án 104:1–2.

should utter that which is meet and seemly, and should refrain from slander, abuse and whatever causeth sadness in men. Lofty is the station of man! Not long ago this exalted Word streamed forth from the treasury of Our Pen of Glory: Great and blessed is this Day—the Day in which all that lay latent in man hath been and will be made manifest. Lofty is the station of man, were he to hold fast to righteousness and truth and to remain firm and steadfast in the Cause. In the eyes of the All-Merciful a true man appeareth even as a firmament; its sun and moon are his sight and hearing, and his shining and resplendent character its stars. His is the loftiest station, and his influence educateth the world of being.

Every receptive soul who hath in this Day inhaled the fragrance of His garment and hath, with a pure heart, set his face towards the all-glorious Horizon is reckoned among the people of Bahá in the Crimson Book. Grasp ye, in My Name, the chalice of My loving-kindness, drink then your fill in My glorious and wondrous remembrance.

O ye that dwell on earth! The religion of God is for love and unity; make it not the cause of enmity or dissension. In the eyes of men of insight and the beholders of the Most Sublime Vision, whatsoever are the effective means for safeguarding and promoting the happiness and welfare of the children of men have already been revealed by the Pen of Glory. But the foolish ones of the earth, being nurtured in evil passions and desires, have remained heedless of the consummate wisdom of Him Who is, in truth, the All-Wise, while their words and deeds are prompted by idle fancies and vain imaginings.

O ye the loved ones and the trustees of God! Kings are the manifestations of the power, and the daysprings of the might and riches, of God. Pray ye on their behalf. He hath invested them with the rulership of the earth and hath singled out the hearts of men as His Own domain.

Conflict and contention are categorically forbidden in His Book. This is a decree of God in this Most Great Revelation. It is divinely preserved from annulment and is invested by Him with the splendour of His confirmation. Verily He is the All-Knowing, the All-Wise.

It is incumbent upon everyone to aid those daysprings of authority and sources of command who are adorned with the ornament of equity and justice. Blessed are the rulers and the learned among the people of Bahá. They are My trustees among My servants and the manifestations of My commandments amidst My people. Upon them rest My glory, My blessings and My grace which have pervaded the world of being. In this connection the utterances revealed in the *Kitáb-i-Aqdas* are such that from the horizon of their words the light of divine grace shineth luminous and resplendent.

O ye My Branches! A mighty force, a consummate power lieth concealed in the world of being. Fix your gaze upon it and upon its unifying influence, and not upon the differences which appear from it.

The Will of the divine Testator is this: It is incumbent upon the Aghsán, the Afnán and My Kindred to turn, one and all, their faces towards the Most Mighty Branch. Consider that which We have revealed in Our Most Holy Book: 'When the ocean of My presence hath ebbed and the Book of My Revelation is ended, turn your faces toward Him Whom God hath purposed, Who hath branched from this Ancient Root.' The object of this sacred verse is none other except the Most Mighty Branch ['Abdu'l-Bahá]. Thus have We graciously revealed unto you our potent Will, and I am verily the Gracious, the All-

Powerful. Verily God hath ordained the station of the Greater Branch [Muḥammad 'Alí] to be beneath that of the Most Great Branch ['Abdu'l-Bahá]. He is in truth the Ordainer, the All-Wise. We have chosen 'the Greater' after 'the Most Great', as decreed by Him Who is the All-Knowing, the All-Informed.

It is enjoined upon everyone to manifest love towards the Aghṣán, but God hath not granted them any right to the property of others.

O ye My Aghṣán, My Afnán and My Kindred! We exhort you to fear God, to perform praiseworthy deeds and to do that which is meet and seemly and serveth to exalt your station. Verily I say, fear of God is the greatest commander that can render the Cause of God victorious, and the hosts which best befit this commander have ever been and are an upright character and pure and goodly deeds.

Say: O servants! Let not the means of order be made the cause of confusion and the instrument of union an occasion for discord. We fain would hope that the people of Bahá may be guided by the blessed words: 'Say: all things are of God.' This exalted utterance is like unto water for quenching the fire of hate and enmity which smouldereth within the hearts and breasts of men. By this single utterance contending peoples and kindreds will attain the light of true unity. Verily He speaketh the truth and leadeth the way. He is the All-Powerful, the Exalted, the Gracious.

It is incumbent upon everyone to show courtesy to, and have regard for the Aghṣán, that thereby the Cause of God may be glorified and His Word exalted. This injunction hath time and again been mentioned and recorded in the Holy Writ. Well is it with him who is enabled to achieve that which the Ordainer, the Ancient of Days hath prescribed for him. Ye are bidden moreover to respect the members of the Holy Household, the Afnán and the kindred. We further admonish you to serve all nations and to strive for the betterment of the world.

That which is conducive to the regeneration of the world and the salvation of the peoples and kindreds of the earth hath been sent down from the heaven of the utterance of Him Who is the Desire of the world. Give ye a hearing ear to the counsels of the Pen of Glory. Better is this for you than all that is on the earth. Unto this beareth witness My glorious and wondrous Book.

16

LAWḤ-I-ARḌ-I-BÁ
(Tablet of the Land of Bá)

PRAISE be to Him Who hath honoured the Land of Bá[1] through the presence of Him round Whom all names revolve. All the atoms of the earth have announced unto all created things that from behind the gate of the Prison-city there hath appeared and above its horizon there hath shone forth the Orb of the beauty of the great, the Most Mighty Branch of God—His ancient and immutable Mystery—proceeding on its way to another land. Sorrow, thereby, hath enveloped this Prison-city, whilst another land rejoiceth. Exalted, immeasurably exalted is our Lord, the Fashioner of the heavens and the Creator of all things, He through Whose sovereignty the doors of the prison were opened, thereby causing what was promised aforetime in the Tablets to be fulfilled. He is verily potent over what He willeth, and in His grasp is the dominion of the entire creation. He is the All-Powerful, the All-Knowing, the All-Wise.

Blessed, doubly blessed, is the ground which His footsteps have trodden, the eye that hath been cheered by the beauty of His countenance, the ear that hath been honoured by hearkening to His call, the heart that hath tasted the sweetness of His love, the breast that hath dilated through

---

[1] Beirut. This Tablet is 'a letter dictated by Bahá'u'lláh and addressed by Mírzá Áqá Ján, His amanuensis, to 'Abdu'l-Bahá while the latter was on a visit to Beirut.' (*The World Order of Bahá'u'lláh*, p. 136.)

His remembrance, the pen that hath voiced His praise, the scroll that hath borne the testimony of His writings. We beseech God—blessed and exalted be He—that He may honour us with meeting Him soon. He is, in truth, the All-Hearing, the All-Powerful, He Who is ready to answer.

17

EXCERPTS FROM OTHER TABLETS

GOD testifieth that there is none other God but Him and that He Who hath come from the heaven of divine revelation is the Hidden Secret, the Impenetrable Mystery, Whose advent hath been foretold in the Book of God and hath been heralded by His Prophets and Messengers. Through Him the mysteries have been unravelled, the veils rent asunder and the signs and evidences disclosed. Lo! He hath now been made manifest. He bringeth to light whatsoever He willeth, and treadeth upon the high places of the earth, invested with transcendent majesty and power.

Blessed is that strong one who will shatter the gods of vain imaginings through the potency of the Name of his Lord, He Who ruleth over all men.

O My Afnán! We would fain mention thy name as a token of grace on Our part, that the sweet savours of My remembrance may attract thee unto My Kingdom and draw thee nigh unto the Tabernacle of My majesty which hath been hoisted through the power of this Name—a Name which hath caused every foundation to tremble.

Say: O peoples of the earth! By the righteousness of God! Whatever ye have been promised in the Books of your Lord, the Ruler of the Day of Return, hath appeared and been made manifest. Beware lest the changes and chances of the world hold you back from Him Who is the Sovereign Truth. Ere long will everything visible perish and only that which hath been revealed by God, the Lord of lords, shall endure.

Say: This is the Day of meritorious deeds, did ye but know it. This is the Day of the glorification of God and of the exposition of His Word, could ye but perceive it. Abandon the things current amongst men and hold fast unto that which God, the Help in Peril, the Self-Subsisting, hath enjoined upon you. The day is fast approaching when all the treasures of the earth shall be of no profit to you. Unto this beareth witness the Lord of Names, He Who proclaimeth: Verily, no God is there besides Him, the Sovereign Truth, the Knower of things unseen.

Well is it with thee, O My Afnán, inasmuch as thou wert honoured to receive My Holy Verses, hast inhaled the sweet savours of My Revelation and responded to My Call at a time when My servants and My creatures, casting the Mother Book behind their backs and, clinging to the dictates of the exponents of idle fancy and vain imaginings, have denounced Me. Thus hath the Tongue of Grandeur spoken in the kingdom of utterance at the bidding of God, the Lord of Creation.

Persevere thou conscientiously in the service of the Cause and, through the power of the Name of thy Lord, the Possessor of all things visible and invisible, preserve the station conferred upon thee. I swear by the righteousness of God! Were anyone apprised of that which is veiled from the eyes of men, he would become so enraptured as to wing his flight unto God, the Lord of all that hath been and shall be.

May His glory rest upon thee and upon such as have drawn nigh unto Him and apprehended the meaning of that which the exalted Pen of God, the Almighty, the All-Loving, hath recorded in this Tablet.

ALL praise be to Thee, O my God, inasmuch as Thou hast adorned the world with the splendour of the dawn following the night wherein was born the One Who heralded the Manifestation of Thy transcendent sovereignty, the Dayspring of Thy divine Essence and the Revelation of Thy supreme Lordship. I beseech Thee, O Creator of the heavens and Fashioner of names, to graciously aid those who have sheltered beneath the shadow of Thine abounding mercy and have raised their voices amidst the peoples of the world for the glorification of Thy Name.

O my God! Thou beholdest the Lord of all mankind confined in His Most Great Prison, calling aloud Thy Name, gazing upon Thy face, proclaiming that which hath enraptured the denizens of Thy kingdoms of revelation and of creation. O my God! I behold Mine own Self captive in the hands of Thy servants, yet the light of Thy sovereignty and the revelations of Thine invincible power shine resplendent from His face, enabling all to know of a certainty that Thou art God, and that there is none other God but Thee. Neither can the power of the powerful frustrate Thee, nor the ascendancy of the rulers prevail against Thee. Thou doest whatsoever Thou willest by virtue of Thy sovereignty which encompasseth all created things, and ordainest that which Thou pleasest through the potency of Thy behest which pervadeth the entire creation.

I implore Thee by the glory of Thy Manifestation and by the power of Thy might, Thy sovereignty and Thine exaltation to render victorious those who have arisen to serve Thee, who have aided Thy Cause and humbled themselves before the splendour of the light of Thy face. Make them then, O my God, triumphant over Thine enemies and cause them to be steadfast in Thy service, that through them the evidences of Thy dominion may be established throughout Thy realms and the tokens of Thine indomitable power be manifested in Thy lands. Verily Thou art potent to do what Thou willest; no God is there but Thee, the Help in Peril, the Self-Subsisting.

This glorious Tablet hath been revealed on the Anniversary of the Birth [of the Báb] that thou mayest recite it in a spirit of humility and supplication and give thanks unto thy Lord, the All-Knowing, the All-Informed. Make thou every effort to render service unto God, that from thee may appear that which will immortalize thy memory in His glorious and exalted heaven.

Say: Glorified art Thou, O my God! I implore Thee by the Dawning-Place of Thy signs and by the Revealer of Thy clear tokens to grant that I may, under all conditions, hold fast the cord of Thy loving providence and cling tenaciously to the hem of Thy generosity. Reckon me then with those whom the changes and chances of the world have failed to deter from serving Thee and from bearing allegiance unto Thee, whom the onslaught of the people hath been powerless to hinder from magnifying Thy Name and celebrating Thy praise. Graciously assist me, O my Lord, to do whatever Thou lovest and desirest. Enable me then to fulfil that which will exalt Thy Name and will set ablaze the fire of Thy love.

Thou art, in truth, the Forgiving, the Bountiful.

O Ḥusayn! God grant thou shalt ever be bright and radiant, beaming with the light of the Sun of Truth, and mayest unloose thy tongue in magnifying the Name of God, which is the most laudable of all acts.

Consider the multitude of souls who seemed to be intensely eager and athirst, yet when the Ocean of living waters did surge forth in the world of being, they remained deprived thereof, inasmuch as they failed to relinquish idle fancy and to become consciously aware of Him Who is the Object of all knowledge. This failure is in recompense for the deeds their hands had formerly wrought.

Render thou thanks unto the Beloved of the world for having graciously aided thee to attain confirmation in this glorious Cause. Entreat Him moreover to make His loved ones steadfast therein, for the inflammatory writings of the mischief-makers are widespread and the clamour of the foreboders of evil is raised high. Happy are they that have cast behind their backs all else save God and have held fast unto that which the Lord of strength and power hath enjoined upon them.

His Glory be upon thee and upon such as have been enabled to recognize and embrace this mighty Cause.

THIS is a Tablet which the Lord of all being hath sent down from His glorious station in honour of him who hath believed in God, the Almighty, the All-Loving.

Blessed is the wayfarer who hath recognized the Desired One, and the seeker who hath heeded the Call of Him Who is the intended Aim of all mankind, and the learned one who hath believed in God, the Help in Peril, the Self-Subsisting.

How vast the number of the learned who have turned

aside from the way of God and how numerous the men devoid of learning who have apprehended the truth and hastened unto Him, saying, 'Praised be Thou, O Lord of all things, visible and invisible.'

By the righteousness of God! The world's horizon is resplendent with the light of the Most Great Luminary, yet the generality of mankind perceive it not. Verily He Who is the Sovereign Truth moveth before the eyes of all men. Unto this beareth witness the One Who is proclaiming in the midmost heart of the world, 'In truth no God is there but Me, Omnipotent over all things, whether of the past or of the future.'

Great is the blessedness of the believer who hath directed himself towards Him and hath gained admittance into His presence, and woe betide every disbeliever who hath turned away from God and followed the wayward and the outcast.

O FRIEND! In the Bayán We directed everyone in this Most Great Revelation to see with his own eyes and hear with his own ears. However when the horizon of the world was illumined with the resplendent light of this Revelation, many people forgot this divine commandment, lost sight of this heavenly exhortation and immersed themselves in the vain imaginings which their minds had devised. Indeed the face of the sun of justice and fairness is hidden behind the clouds of idle fancy which the foolish ones have conceived. Therefore it is not to be wondered at that the movements of the birds of darkness attract attention. Through the potency of the Name of the Best-Beloved, invite thou the receptive souls unto God's holy court, that perchance they may not remain deprived of the heavenly Fountain of living water. He is in truth the Gracious, the Forgiving.

The gaze of the loving-kindness of God—exalted and glorified is He—hath everlastingly been directed towards His beloved friends; verily He is the One Who knoweth and remembereth.

O Javád! Such is the greatness of this Day that the Hour itself is seized with perturbation, and all heavenly Scriptures bear evidence to its overpowering majesty. In this Day the Book solemnly testifieth to His glory and the Balance is moved to lift up its voice. This is the Day wherein the Ṣiráṭ calleth aloud: 'I am the straight Path', and Mount Sinai exclaimeth: 'Verily the Lord of Revelation is come.'

Being overcome by the drunkenness of corrupt inclinations, the people of the earth find themselves in a state of stupor. They are, therefore, debarred from the wondrous signs of God, are prevented from attaining the ultimate goal and are deprived of the liberal effusions of divine grace.

It behoveth the people of God to be forbearing. They should impart the Word of God according to the hearer's particular measure of understanding and capacity, that perchance the children of men may be roused from heedlessness and set their faces towards this Horizon which is immeasurably exalted above every horizon.

O Javád! The manifold bounties of God have ever been and will continue to be vouchsafed unto thee. Praised be God! Thou hast been shielded from the most great terror and hast succeeded in drawing nigh unto the Most Great Bounty at a time when all men were prevented from recognizing the eternal King by the interposition of the veils of outward glory, namely the divines of this day. Cherish thou as dearly as thine own life this testimony pronounced by the All-Glorious Pen and strive with all thy might to preserve it by the potency of the Name of Him Who is the Beloved One of the entire creation, that this sublime honour may be proof against the eyes and the hands of robbers. Verily thy Lord is the Expounder, the All-Knowing.

Convey the greetings of this Wronged One unto all the beloved friends in that region and call to their minds Our wondrous and exalted remembrances, that haply they may forsake the things current amongst them, may set their hearts on that which pertaineth unto God and remain purged from unseemly deeds and pursuits.

May the glory of the Almighty, the All-Wise, be upon thee and upon such as are related unto thee.

WE make mention of him who hath been attracted by Our Call when it was raised from the summit of transcendent glory and hath set his face towards God, the Lord of creation. He is numbered with such as have heard and responded to the summons of their Lord at a time when the peoples of the world are wrapt in palpable veils. He testifieth unto that whereunto God hath testified, and acknowledgeth his belief in that which the Tongue of Grandeur hath uttered. Unto this beareth witness the Lord of Names in this wondrous Tablet.

O My exalted Pen! Bring him, on My behalf, the joyful tidings concerning the things that God, the Powerful, the Omnipotent, hath reserved for him. Indeed he hath, for most of the time, been hemmed in by manifold sorrows, and verily his merciful Lord is the One Who seeth and knoweth all things. Rejoice thou with exceeding gladness inasmuch as this Wronged One hath turned His face towards thee, hath mentioned thy name aforetime and doth mention it at this very moment.

Unto My loved friends give thou remembrances in My Name and convey to them the tidings of the gracious bounties of their Lord, the Giver, the All-Generous. From this exalted station We send Our greetings unto such believers as have taken fast hold on the Sure Handle and quaffed the choice wine of constancy from the hand of favour of their Lord, the Almighty, the All-Praised.

In this Day the faculty of hearing exclaimeth, 'This is my Day, wherein I hearken unto the wondrous Voice coming from the precincts of the Prison of my Lord, the Perspicuous, the Hearing.' And the faculty of sight calleth aloud, 'Verily this is my Day, for I behold the Dayspring of glory shining resplendent at the bidding of Him Who is the Ordainer, the All-Powerful.' Blessed the ear that hath heard the call, 'Behold, and thou shalt see Me.'[1] and happy the eye that hath gazed upon the most wondrous Sign, dawning from this luminous horizon.

Say: O concourse of the rulers and of the learned and the wise! The Promised Day is come and the Lord of Hosts hath appeared. Rejoice ye with great joy by reason of this supreme felicity. Aid Him then through the power of wisdom and utterance. Thus biddeth you the One Who

[1] Qur'án 7:139.

hath ever proclaimed, 'Verily, no God is there but Me, the All-Knowing, the All-Wise.'

May His glory rest upon thee and upon those who are with thee and such ones as cherish thee and give ear to the words thou utterest in glorification of this mighty, this transcendent Revelation.

O THOU who bearest My Name, Júd[1] [Bounty]! Upon thee be My Glory. Give ear unto that which thou didst hear aforetime when the Day-Star of testimony was shining resplendent above the horizon of 'Iráq, when Baghdád served as the Seat of the Throne of thy Lord, the Exalted, the Mighty.

I bear witness that thou hast hearkened unto the melody of God and His sweet accents, inclined thine ear to the cooing of the Dove of divine Revelation and hast heard the Nightingale of fidelity pouring forth its notes upon the Branch of Glory: Verily there is none other God but Me, the Incomparable, the All-Informed.

O thou who bearest My Name! The glances of the loving-kindness of God have been and continue to be directed towards thee. While in His presence, thou hast heard the Voice of the One true God—exalted be His glory—and hast beheld the unveiled splendour of the Light of divine knowledge. Ponder a while! How sublime is the Utterance of Him Who is the Sovereign Truth and how abject are the idle contentions of the people! The accumulations of vain fancy have obstructed men's ears and stopped them from hearing the Voice of God, and the veils of

[1] See footnote p. 74.

human learning and false imaginings have prevented their eyes from beholding the splendour of the light of His countenance. With the arm of might and power We have rescued a number of souls from the slough of impending extinction and enabled them to attain the Dayspring of glory. Moreover We have laid bare the divine mysteries and in most explicit language foretold future events, that neither the doubts of the faithless, nor the denials of the froward, nor the whisperings of the heedless may keep back the seekers of truth from the Source of the light of the One true God. Nevertheless some people seem to have been seized with epilepsy, others are torn up even as hollow tree-stumps. They abandon God, the Most Exalted —He before Whose revelation of a single verse, all the Scriptures of the past and of more recent times pale into lowliness and insignificance—and set their hearts on lving tales and follow empty words.

Thou hast surely quaffed from the ocean of Mine utterance and hast witnessed the effulgent splendour of the orb of My wisdom. Thou hast also heard the sayings of the infidels who neither are acquainted with the fundamentals of the Faith, nor have tasted this choice Wine whose seal hath been broken through the power of My Name, the Help in Peril, the Self-Subsisting. Beseech thou God that the believers who are endued with true understanding may be graciously enabled to do that which is pleasing unto Him.

How strange that despite this ringing Call, despite the appearance of this most wondrous Revelation, We notice that men, for the most part, have fixed their hearts on the vanities of the world and are sorely dismayed and troubled by reason of prevailing doubts and evil suggestions. Say: This is the Day of God Himself; fear ye God and be not of them that have disbelieved in Him. Cast the idle tales behind your backs and behold My Revelation through Mine eyes. Unto this have ye been exhorted in heavenly Books and Scriptures, in the Scrolls and Tablets.

Arise thou to serve the Cause of thy Lord; then give the people the joyful tidings concerning this resplendent Light whose revelation hath been announced by God through His Prophets and Messengers. Admonish everyone moreover to observe prudence as ordained by Him, and in the Name of God advise them, saying: It behoveth every one in this Day of God to dedicate himself to the teaching of the Cause with utmost prudence and steadfastness. Should he discover a pure soil, let him sow the seed of the Word of God, otherwise it would be preferable to observe silence.

Not long ago this most sublime Word was revealed in the Crimson Book by the All-Glorious Pen: 'The heaven of divine wisdom is illumined with two luminaries: consultation and compassion.' Please God, everyone may be enabled to observe this weighty and blessed word.

Certain people seem to be entirely bereft of understanding. By clinging to the cord of idle fancy they have debarred themselves from the Sure Handle. I swear by My life! Were they to reflect a while with fairness on that which the All-Merciful hath sent down, they would, one and all, spontaneously give utterance to these words, 'Verily Thou art the Truth, the manifest Truth.'

It behoveth thee to turn thy gaze in all circumstances unto the One true God, and seek diligently to serve His Cause. Call thou to mind when thou wert in My company, within the Tabernacle of Glory, and didst hear from Me that which He Who conversed with God [Moses] heard upon the Sinai of divine knowledge. Thus did We graciously aid thee, enabled thee to recognize the truth and cautioned thee, that thou mightest render thanks unto thy bountiful Lord. Thou shouldst safeguard this sublime station through the potency of My Name, the Omnipotent, the Faithful.

Convey greetings on My behalf to My loved ones and suffer them to hearken unto My sweet Voice. Thus biddeth thee the One Who hath bidden thee in the past; I am in truth the Ordainer, the All-Informed. Glory be upon thee and upon those who give ear to thy words concerning this momentous Cause and who love thee for the sake of God, the Lord of the worlds.

O Ḥaydar![1] This Wronged One hath heard thy voice raised in the service of the Cause of God and is well aware of the feeling of joy which His love hath roused in thy heart and of thy pangs of anguish at that which hath befallen His loved ones. I swear by the Lord of mercy! The whole world is overwhelmed with sorrow whilst mankind is perplexed with doubts and dissensions. The people of God, the Lord of Names, are so grievously beset by enemies that the supreme Paradise hath lamented and the inmates of highest Heaven and those who, day and night, circle round the Throne have groaned aloud.

O 'Alí! Woes and sorrows are powerless to restrain thy Lord, the All-Merciful. Indeed He hath risen to champion the Cause of God in such wise that neither the overpowering might of the world nor the tyranny of the nations can ever alarm Him. He calleth aloud betwixt earth and

[1] See footnote 1 on page 57.

heaven, saying: The Promised Day is come. The Lord of creation proclaimeth: Verily, there is no God besides Me, the Almighty, the All-Bountiful.

O 'Alí! The immature wish to put out the light of God with their mouths and to extinguish by their acts the flame in the Burning Bush. Say, wretched indeed is your plight, O ye embodiments of delusion. Fear ye God and reject not the heavenly grace which hath shed radiance upon all regions. Say, He Who is the Exponent of the hidden Name hath appeared, did ye but know it. He Whose advent hath been foretold in the heavenly Scriptures is come, could ye but understand it. The world's horizon is illumined by the splendours of this Most Great Revelation. Haste ye with radiant hearts and be not of them that are bereft of understanding. The appointed Hour hath struck and mankind is laid low. Unto this bear witness the honoured servants of God.

O Ḥaydar-'Alí! I swear by the righteousness of God! The Blast hath been blown on the Trumpet of the Bayán as decreed by the Lord, the Merciful, and all that are in the heavens and on the earth have swooned away except such as have detached themselves from the world, cleaving fast unto the Cord of God, the Lord of mankind. This is the Day in which the earth shineth with the effulgent light of thy Lord, but the people are lost in error and have been shut out as by a veil. We desire to regenerate the world, yet they have resolved to put an end to My life. Thus have their hearts prompted them in this Day—a Day which hath been made bright by the radiant light of the countenance of its Lord, the Omnipotent, the Almighty, the Unconstrained. The Mother Book hath lifted up its Voice, but the people are bereft of hearing. The Preserved Tablet hath been revealed with truth, yet the generality of mankind peruse it not. They have denied the gracious favour of God after it hath been sent down unto them and have turned away from God, the Knower of things unseen. They firmly cling to the hem of idle fancies, turning their backs on the hidden Name of the Almighty.

Say, O concourse of divines! Be fair in your judgement, I adjure you by God. Produce then whatever proofs and testimonies ye possess, if ye are to be reckoned among the inmates of this glorious habitation. Set your hearts towards the Dayspring of divine Revelation that We may disclose before your eyes the equivalent of all such verses, proofs, testimonies, affirmations and evidences as ye and other kindreds of the earth possess. Fear ye God and be not of them that well deserve the chastisement of God, the Lord of creation.

This is the Day in which the Ocean of knowledge hath lifted up its Voice and hath brought forth its pearls. Would that ye knew it! The heaven of the Bayán hath been raised up in truth at the behest of God, the Help in Peril, the Self-Subsisting. I swear by God! The Essence of knowledge exclaimeth and saith: Lo! He Who is the Object of all knowledge is come and through His advent the sacred Books of God, the Gracious, the Loving, have been embellished. Every revelation of grace, every evidence of goodly gifts emanateth from Him and unto Him doth it return.

Fear ye God, O concourse of the foolish, and do not inflict tribulations upon those who have willed naught but that which God hath willed. Moreover, if ye heed my call, follow not your selfish desires. The day is approaching when everything now discernible will have faded away and ye shall weep for having failed in your duty towards God. Unto this testifieth this inscribed Tablet.

Rejoice thou with great joy that We have remembered thee both now and in the past. Indeed the sweet savours of this remembrance shall endure and shall not change throughout the eternity of the Names of God, the Lord of mankind. We have graciously accepted thy devotions, thy praise, thy teaching work and the services thou hast rendered for the sake of this mighty Announcement. We have also hearkened unto that which thy tongue hath uttered at the meetings and gatherings. Verily thy Lord heareth and observeth all things. We have attired thee with the vesture of My good-pleasure in My heavenly Kingdom, and from the Divine Lote-Tree which is raised on the borders of the vale of security and peace, situate in the luminous Spot beyond the glorious City, We call aloud unto thee saying: In truth there is no God but Me, the All-Knowing, the All-Wise. We have brought thee into being to serve Me, to glorify My Word and to proclaim My Cause. Centre thine energies upon that wherefor thou hast been created by virtue of the Will of the supreme Ordainer, the Ancient of Days.

At this moment We call to remembrance Our loved ones and bring them the joyous tidings of God's unfailing grace and of the things that have been provided for them in My lucid Book. Ye have tolerated the censure of the enemies for the sake of My love and have steadfastly endured in My Path the grievous cruelties which the ungodly have inflicted upon you. Unto this I Myself bear witness, and I am the All-Knowing. How vast the number of places that have been ennobled with your blood for the sake of God. How numerous the cities wherein the voice of your lamentation hath been raised and the wailing of your anguish uplifted. How many the prisons into which ye have been cast by the hosts of tyranny. Know ye of a certainty that He will render you victorious, will exalt you among the peoples of the world and will demonstrate your high rank before the gaze of all nations. Surely He will not suffer the reward of His favoured ones to be lost.

Take heed lest the deeds wrought by the embodiments of idle fancy sadden you or the acts committed by every wayward oppressor grieve you. Seize ye the chalice of constancy through the power of His Name, quaff then therefrom by virtue of the sovereignty of God, the Powerful, the Omnipotent. Thus hath the Day-Star of My tender compassion and loving-kindness shone forth above the horizon of this Tablet that ye may render thanks unto your Lord, the Almighty, the All-Bountiful.

The glory that hath dawned resplendent from the heaven of Mine utterance rest upon thee and upon them that have directed themselves towards thee and inclined their ears to the words which thy mouth hath uttered concerning this glorious, this august Revelation.

By the righteousness of God! The Mother Book is made manifest, summoning mankind unto God, the Lord of the worlds, while the seas proclaim: The Most Great Ocean hath appeared, from whose waves one can hear the thundering cry: 'Verily, no God is there but Me, the Peerless, the All-Knowing.' And the trees raising their clamour exclaim: O people of the world! The voice of the Divine Lote-Tree is clearly sounding and the shrill cry of the Pen of Glory is ringing loud: Give ye ear and be not of the heedless. The sun is calling out: O concourse of the divines! The heaven of religions is split and the moon cleft asunder and the peoples of the earth are brought together in a new resurrection. Fear ye God and follow not the promptings of your passions, rather follow Him unto Whom have testified the Scriptures of God, the All-Knowing, the All-Wise.

The episode of Sinai hath been re-enacted in this Revelation and He Who conversed upon the Mount is calling aloud: Verily, the Desired One is come, seated upon the throne of certitude, could ye but perceive it. He hath admonished all men to observe that which is conducive to the exaltation of the Cause of God and will guide mankind unto His Straight Path.

How vast the number of the down-trodden who have been enraptured by the Call of God! How numerous the potentates who have risen up to commit acts of aggression that have caused the inmates of the all-highest Paradise to lament and the dwellers of this glorious habitation to wail with grief! How great the multitude of the poor who have quaffed the choice wine of divine revelation and how many the rich who have turned away, repudiated the truth and voiced their disbelief in God, the Lord of this blessed and wondrous Day!

Say: Fear ye God, then observe equity in your judgement of this Great Announcement before which, as soon as it shone forth, every momentous announcement bowed low in adoration. Say: O concourse of the foolish! If ye reject Him, by what evidence can ye prove your allegiance to the former Messengers of God or vindicate your belief in that which He hath sent down from His mighty and exalted Kingdom? What benefit do your possessions bestow upon you? What protection can your treasures afford you? None, I swear by the Spirit of God that pervadeth all that are in the heavens and on the earth. Cast away that which ye have put together with the hands of idle fancy and vain imaginings and take fast hold of the Book of God which hath been sent down by virtue of His all-compelling and inviolable authority.

Thy letter was presented before this Wronged One and in thine honour have We revealed this Tablet from which the fragrance of the gracious favour of thy Lord, the Compassionate, the Bountiful, is diffused. We beseech God to make thee as a banner upraised in the city of His remembrance, and to exalt thy station in this Cause—a Cause beneath whose shadow the sincere ones of God shall behold the peoples and kindreds of the earth seeking shelter. Verily, thy Lord knoweth and informeth. Moreover We entreat Him to nourish thee with the best of what hath been treasured in His Book. He is in truth the One Who doth hear and answer the call.

Persevere thou in helping His Cause through the strengthening power of the hosts of wisdom and utterance. Thus hath it been decreed by God, the Gracious, the All-Praised. Blessed is the believer who hath in this Day embraced the Truth and the man of fixed resolve whom the hosts of tyranny have been powerless to affright.

The glory which hath shone forth above the horizon of utterance be upon thee and upon such believers as have seized the chalice of His sealed wine through the power of His Name, the Self-Subsisting, and drunk deep despite those that have rejected the One in Whom they had formerly professed belief—they that have disputed the truth of this Great Announcement whereunto God hath testified in His precious and ancient Book.

O MUHAMMAD Husayn! Be thou prepared to receive the outpourings of the loving-kindness of God, the Lord of the worlds. The All-Merciful hath deigned to bestow upon thee pearls of knowledge from the Ocean of the grace of God, the Almighty, the Most Exalted.

Where is the man of insight who will recognize and perceive the truth? Where is to be found the man of hearing who will hearken unto My wondrous Voice calling from the realm of glory? Where is the soul who will set his face towards the Divine Lote-Tree in such wise that neither the overpowering might of the kings, nor the violent commotions of their subjects may frustrate him, lifting up his voice amidst the entire creation through the power of wisdom and utterance and testifying unto that whereunto hath testified God, that verily no God is there besides Him, the Powerful, the Invincible, the Omnipotent, the Knowing, the Wise.

O Husayn! Thy name hath been mentioned in the Most Great Prison before this Wronged One and We have revealed for thee that with which none of the books of the world can compare. Unto this beareth witness the King of eternity; yet the generality of mankind are numbered among the heedless. From the dawning-place of testimony We have raised the Call unto all that dwell in the realm of creation. Amongst men there are those who have been carried away by the fragrance of the utterance of their Lord in such manner that they have forsaken everything which pertaineth unto men in their eagerness to attain the court of the presence of God, the Lord of the mighty throne. There are also those who are sore perplexed and wavering. Others have made haste, winged their way to answer the Call of their Lord, the Ancient of Days. Still others have turned aside, rejected the truth and eventually disbelieved in God, the Almighty, the All-Praised. And there are yet others who have pronounced judgement against Him with such cruelty that every wise and discerning soul hath been moved to lament. We have graciously summoned them unto the river that is life indeed, while they have, with manifest injustice, decreed the shedding of My blood. Thus hath the Day-Star of wisdom shone forth from above the horizon of the utterance of thy Lord, the All-Merciful. Shouldst thou attain unto its light, it behoveth thee to magnify the praise of thy Lord and say, I yield Thee thanks, O God of the worlds.

Blessed art thou and are they whom the world and its vanities have failed to deter from this luminous Horizon.

Convey greetings on My behalf unto My loved ones. We exhort them to observe wisdom as decreed in My wondrous Book.

O My handmaiden and My leaf! Rejoice with great joy inasmuch as thy call hath ascended unto the Divine Lote-Tree and is answered from the all-glorious Horizon. Verily, no God is there but Me, the Wronged One, the Exile.

We have revealed Ourself unto men, have unveiled the Cause, guided all mankind towards God's Straight Path, promulgated the laws and have enjoined upon everyone that which shall truly profit them both in this world and in the next; yet they have pronounced judgement to shed My blood, whereat the Maid of Heaven hath wept sore, Sinai hath lamented and the Faithful Spirit was made to sigh with grief.

In these days the people have debarred themselves from the effusions of divine grace by following in the footsteps of every ignorant one that hath gone astray. They have cast the Ocean of divine knowledge behind their backs and fixed their eyes upon such foolish men as claim to be well versed in learning without being supported by any evidence from God, the Lord of mankind.

Well is it with thee inasmuch as thou hast forsaken idle imaginings and taken fast hold of the Cord of God that no man can sever. Consider the gracious favour of God—exalted be His glory. How numerous are the kings and queens on earth who, despite much yearning, anticipation and waiting, have been debarred from Him Who is the Desire of the world, whilst thou didst attain. God willing, thou mayest accomplish a deed whose fragrance shall endure as long as the Names of God—exalted be His glory —will endure. By the righteousness of God! The title 'O My handmaiden' far excelleth aught else that can be seen in the world. Ere long the eyes of mankind shall be illumined and cheered by recognizing that which Our Pen of Glory hath revealed.

Blessed art thou and blessed is the mother that hath nursed thee. Appreciate the value of this station and arise to serve His Cause in such wise that the idle fancies and insinuations of the doubters withhold thee not from this high resolve. The Day-Star of certitude is shining resplendent but the people of the world are holding fast unto vain imaginings. The Ocean of divine knowledge hath risen high whilst the children of men are clinging to the hem of the foolish. But for the unfailing grace of God—exalted be His glory—no antidote could ever cure these inveterate diseases.

Convey My greetings unto the handmaidens of God in

that region and give them the joyful tidings that His tender mercy and grace are vouchsafed unto them. High indeed is the station We have destined for thee. It behoveth thee to yield praise and thanksgiving unto thy Lord, the Bountiful, the Most Generous. Glorified be God, the Exalted, the Great.

At one time this sublime Word was heard from the Tongue of Him Who is the Possessor of all being and the Lord of the throne on high and of earth below—exalted is the glory of His utterance—: Piety and detachment are even as two most great luminaries of the heaven of teaching. Blessed the one who hath attained unto this supreme station, this habitation of transcendent holiness and sublimity.

This is a Tablet sent down by the All-Merciful from the Kingdom of utterance unto all that dwell on earth. Happy is the man who hearkeneth and heedeth and woe betide him who hath erred and doubted. This is the Day that hath been illumined by the effulgent light of the Countenance of God—the Day when the Tongue of Grandeur is calling aloud: The Kingdom is God's, the Lord of the Day of Resurrection.

Thy name hath been mentioned in Our Presence and We have deigned to reveal for thee that which the tongue of no one among the peoples of the world can recount. Rejoice with exceeding joy inasmuch as thou hast been remembered in the Most Great Prison and the Countenance of the Ancient of Days hath turned towards thee from this exalted habitation.

We have truly revealed the signs, demonstrated the irrefutable testimonies and have summoned all men unto the straight Path. Among the people there are those who have turned away and repudiated the truth, others have pronounced judgement against Us without any proof or evidence. The first to turn away from Us have been the world's spiritual leaders in this age—they that call upon Us in the daytime and in the night season and mention My Name while resting on their lofty thrones. However, when I revealed Myself unto men they rose against Me in such wise that even the stones groaned and lamented bitterly.

Great is thy blessedness inasmuch as thou hast hearkened unto His Voice, set thy face towards Him and heeded the Call of thy Lord when He came invested with invincible power and sovereignty.

O My handmaiden, O My leaf! Render thou thanks unto the Best-Beloved of the world for having attained this boundless grace at a time when the world's learned and most distinguished men have remained deprived thereof. We have designated thee 'a leaf' that thou mayest, like unto leaves, be stirred by the gentle wind of the Will of God— exalted be His glory—even as the leaves of the trees are stirred by onrushing winds. Yield thou thanks unto thy Lord by virtue of this brilliant utterance. Wert thou to perceive the sweetness of the title 'O My handmaiden' thou wouldst find thyself detached from all mankind, devoutly engaged day and night in communion with Him Who is the sole Desire of the world.

In words of incomparable beauty We have made fitting mention of such leaves and handmaidens as have quaffed from the living waters of heavenly grace and have kept their eyes directed towards God. Happy and blessed are they indeed. Ere long shall God reveal their station whose loftiness no word can befittingly express nor any description adequately describe.

We admonish thee to do that which will serve to promote the interests of the Cause of God amongst men and women. He doth hear the call of the friends and beholdeth their actions. Verily, He is the Hearing and the Seeing.

Upon thee and upon them be the glory of God, the Powerful, the All-Knowing, the All-Wise.

O HANDMAID of God! Hearken unto the Voice of the Lord of Names, Who from His Prison hath directed His gaze towards thee and is making mention of thee.

He hath extended assistance to every wayfarer, hath graciously responded to every petitioner and granted admittance to every seeker after truth. In this Day the Straight Path is made manifest, the Balance of divine justice is set and the light of the sun of His bounty is resplendent, yet the oppressive darkness of the people of tyranny hath, even as clouds, intervened and caused a grievous obstruction between the Day-Star of heavenly grace and the people of the world. Blessed is he who hath rent the intervening veils asunder and is illumined by the radiant light of divine Revelation. Consider how numerous were those who accounted themselves among the wise and the learned, yet in the Day of God were deprived of the outpourings of heavenly bounties.

O My leaf, O My handmaid! Appreciate the value of this blessing and of this tender mercy which hath encompassed thee and guided thy steps unto the Dayspring of glory.

Convey greetings on behalf of this Wronged One to such handmaidens as worship God and cheer their hearts with the assurance of His loving providence.

Fix your gaze upon wisdom in all things, for it is an unfailing antidote. How often hath it turned a disbeliever into a believer or a foe into a friend? Its observance is highly essential, inasmuch as this theme hath been set forth in numerous Tablets revealed from the empyrean of the Will of Him Who is the Manifestation of the light of divine unity. Well is it with them that act accordingly.

Centre your attention unceasingly upon that which will cause the Word of God to be exalted. In this Most Great Revelation goodly deeds and a praiseworthy character are regarded as the hosts of God, likewise is His blessed and holy Word. These hosts are the lodestone of the hearts of men and the effective means for unlocking doors. Of all the weapons in the world this is the keenest.

Beseech thou God to graciously assist all men to observe that which His all-glorious Pen hath recorded in the sacred Books and Tablets.

THIS Wronged One doth mention him who hath set his face toward the Incomparable One, the All-Knowing, him who beareth witness unto His unity even as the All-Glorious Pen hath borne witness as it moveth swiftly within the arena of utterance. Blessed is the soul that hath recognized its Lord and woe betide him who hath grievously erred and doubted.

Man is like unto a tree. If he be adorned with fruit, he hath been and will ever be worthy of praise and commendation. Otherwise a fruitless tree is but fit for fire. The fruits of the human tree are exquisite, highly desired and dearly cherished. Among them are upright character, virtuous deeds and a goodly utterance. The springtime for earthly trees occurreth once every year, while the one for human trees appeareth in the Days of God—exalted be His glory. Were the trees of men's lives to be adorned in this divine Springtime with the fruits that have been mentioned, the effulgence of the light of Justice would, of a certainty, illumine all the dwellers of the earth and everyone would abide in tranquillity and contentment beneath the sheltering shadow of Him Who is the Object of all mankind. The Water for these trees is the living water of the sacred Words uttered by the Beloved of the world. In one instant are such trees planted and in the next their branches shall, through the outpourings of the showers of divine mercy, have reached the skies. A dried-up tree, however, hath never been nor will be worthy of any mention.

Happy is the faithful one who is attired with the vesture of high endeavour and hath arisen to serve this Cause. Such a soul hath truly attained the desired Goal and hath apprehended the Object for which it hath been created. But a myriad times alas for the wayward who are like unto dried-up leaves fallen upon the dust. Ere long mortal blasts shall carry them away to the place ordained for them. Ignorant did they arrive, ignorant did they linger and ignorant did they retire to their abodes.

The world is continually proclaiming these words: Beware, I am evanescent, and so are all my outward appearances and colours. Take ye heed of the changes and chances contrived within me and be ye roused from your slumber. Nevertheless there is no discerning eye to see, nor is there a hearing ear to hearken.

In this Day the inner ear exclaimeth and saith: Indeed well is it with me, today is my day, inasmuch as the Voice of God is calling aloud. And the essence of vision crieth out: Blessed am I, this is my day, for the Ancient Beauty is shining resplendent from the most exalted Horizon.

It behoveth the people of Bahá to invoke and entreat the Lord of Names that perchance the people of the world may not be deprived of the effusions of grace in His days.

In the past the divines were perplexed over this question, a question which He Who is the Sovereign Truth hath, during the early years of His life, Himself heard them ask repeatedly: 'What is that Word which the Qá'im will pronounce whereby the leaders of religion are put to flight?' Say, that Word is now made manifest and ye have fled ere ye heard it uttered, although ye perceive it not. And that blessed, that hidden, that concealed and treasured Word is this: '"HE" hath now appeared in the raiment of "I". He Who was hidden from mortal eyes exclaimeth: Lo! I am the All-Manifest.' This is the Word which hath caused the limbs of disbelievers to quake. Glorified be God! All the heavenly Scriptures of the past attest to the greatness of this Day, the greatness of this Manifestation, the greatness of His signs, the greatness of His Word, the greatness of His constancy, the greatness of His pre-eminent station. Yet despite all this the people have remained heedless and are shut out as by a veil. Indeed all the Prophets have yearned to attain this Day. David saith: 'Who will bring me into the Strong City?'[1] By Strong City is meant 'Akká. Its fortifications are very strong and this Wronged One is imprisoned within its walls. Likewise it is revealed in the Qur'án: 'Bring forth thy people from the darkness into the light and announce to them the days of God.'[2]

The glory with which this Day is invested hath been explicitly mentioned and clearly set forth in most heavenly Books and Scriptures. However, the divines of the age have debarred men from this transcendent station, and have kept them back from this Pinnacle of Glory, this Supreme Goal.

Blessed art thou inasmuch as the darkness of vain imaginings hath been powerless to hinder thee from the light of certitude, and the onslaught of the people hath failed to deter thee from the Lord of mankind. Appreciate thou the value of this high station and beseech God— exalted is His glory—to graciously enable thee to safeguard it. Imperishable dominion hath exclusively pertained unto the One true God and His loved ones and will continue to pertain unto them everlastingly.

The glory that hath shone forth from the horizon of eternity rest upon thee and upon such as have taken fast hold of the Cord of God that no man can sever.

HE Who leadeth to true victory is come. By the righteousness of God! He is fully capable of revolutionizing the

[1] Psalms 59:9; 108:10.
[2] Qur'án 14:5.

world through the power of a single Word. Having enjoined upon all men to observe wisdom, He Himself hath adhered to the cord of patience and resignation.

The clay clods of the world have set forth to visit the embellished, the luminous, the crimson City of God, and certain emissaries from Persia are secretly stirring up mischief, though to outward seeming they pretend to be gentle and meek. Gracious God! When will this world-afflicting craftiness be transformed into sincerity? The exhortations of God, the True One, have compassed the world, but until now their influence hath not been disclosed. Men's unseemly deeds have kept them back from attaining unto Him. We entreat God—exalted and glorified is He—to pour down, out of the clouds of divine grace, the overflowing rain of His bounty upon all His servants. Verily potent is He over all things.

O 'Alí Ḥaydar! O thou who hast risen to serve My Cause and art engaged in magnifying the praise of God, the Lord of the mighty throne! Unto the emblems of justice and the exponents of equity it is indubitably clear and evident that this Wronged One, strengthened by the transcendent power of the Kingdom, is seeking to efface from among the peoples and kindreds of the earth every evidence of disorder, discord, dissension, differences or divisions; and it is for no other reason but this great, this momentous object that He hath again and again been cast into prison and many a day and a night hath been subjected to chains and fetters. Blessed are they that judge this impregnable Cause, this glorious Announcement, with fairness and equity.

This is a Tablet sent down by the Lord of mercy that the people of the world may be enabled to draw nigh unto this Ocean which hath surged through the potency of His august Name. Amongst men there are those who have turned away from Him and gainsaid His testimony, while others have quaffed the wine of assurance in the glory of His Name which pervadeth all created things. A grievous loss hath indeed been suffered by those that have inclined their ears to the croaking of the raven, and refused to hearken unto the sweet warblings of the Bird of Heaven singing upon the twigs of the Tree of eternity: Verily there is none other God but Me, the All-Knowing, the All-Wise. This is the Day that hath been illumined by the splendours of the light of Our countenance—the Day around which all days and nights circle in adoration. Blessed is the man of insight who hath perceived, and the sore athirst who hath quaffed from this luminous Fountain. Blessed the man who acknowledgeth the truth, earnestly striving to serve the Cause of his Lord, the Powerful, the Almighty.

O servant who hast fixed his gaze upon My face! Hearken unto the Voice of thy Lord, the All-Glorious, calling aloud from the dayspring of grandeur and majesty. Verily His Call will draw thee nigh unto the realm of glory and will cause thee to extol His praise in such wise that every created thing will be enraptured, and to magnify His glory in such manner as to influence the entire creation. Truly thy Lord is the Protector, the Gracious, the All-Informed.

Gather thou together the friends of God in that land and acquaint them with My incomparable remembrance. We have revealed for them a Tablet from which the fragrance of the All-Merciful hath been wafted upon the realm of existence, that they may rejoice with exceeding gladness and remain steadfast in this wondrous Cause.

While in prison We have revealed a Book which We have entitled 'The Most Holy Book'. We have enacted laws therein and adorned it with the commandments of thy Lord, Who exerciseth authority over all that are in the heavens and on the earth. Say: Take hold of it, O people, and observe that which hath been sent down in it of the wondrous precepts of your Lord, the Forgiving, the Bountiful. It will truly prosper you both in this world and in the next and will purge you of whatsoever ill beseemeth you. He is indeed the Ordainer, the Expounder, the Giver, the Generous, the Gracious, the All-Praised.

Great is thy blessedness inasmuch as thou hast been faithful to the Covenant of God and His Testament and for thy being honoured with this Tablet through which thy name is recorded in My Preserved Tablet. Dedicate thyself to the service of the Cause of thy Lord, cherish His remembrance in thy heart and celebrate His praise in such wise that every wayward and heedless soul may thereby be roused from slumber.

Thus have We deigned to bestow upon thee a token of favour from Our presence; and I verily am the Forgiving, the All-Merciful.

WE desire to mention him who hath set his face towards Us and to let him once again drink deep from the life-giving waters of Our gracious providence that he may be enabled to draw nigh unto My Horizon, be adorned with Mine attributes, soar in Mine atmosphere, be confirmed in that which will cause the sanctity of My Cause to be manifested amongst My people and to celebrate My praise in a manner that will cause every hesitating soul to hasten, every motionless creature to wing its flight, every mortal frame to be consumed, every chilled heart to be stirred with life and every dejected spirit to surge with delight. Thus doth it behove him who hath turned his face to Mine, hath entered beneath the shadow of My loving-kindness and received My verses which have pervaded the whole world.

O 'Alí! He Who is the Dayspring of divine Revelation is calling unto thee through this most wondrous utterance. By the righteousness of God! If thou wert present before My Throne and didst hearken unto the Tongue of might and grandeur, thou wouldst sacrifice thy body, thy soul, thine entire being as a token of thy love for God, the Sovereign, the Protector, the All-Knowing, the All-Wise, and wouldst so thrill to the fascination of His Voice that every pen would be powerless to recount thy station and every eloquent speaker would be confounded in his attempt to describe it. Ponder a while concerning this Revelation and its invincible sovereignty; aid it then as it beseemeth thy Lord, the Gracious, the All-Bountiful. Direct thou the people unto the Dayspring of glory. Verily it is He Himself Who is established upon His mighty Throne. Through Him hath the horizon of this Prison been made to shine and by Him have all that are in the heavens and on the earth been illumined.

We have deigned to mention thy name in the past as well as in this gracious Tablet that thou mayest once again inhale the sweet fragrance of the All-Merciful. This is but a token of My favour unto thee. Render thou thanks unto thy Lord, the All-Bountiful, the All-Seeing.

Grieve thou not at men's failure to apprehend the Truth.

Ere long thou shalt find them turning towards God, the Lord of all mankind. We have indeed, through the potency of the Most Sublime Word, encompassed the whole world, and the time is approaching when God will have subdued the hearts of all that dwell on earth. He is in truth the Omnipotent, the All-Powerful.

We also remember thy brother from this land that he may rejoice at My mention of him and be of them that reflect.

O friend! The Best-Beloved is calling thee from His Most Great Prison and exhorteth thee to observe that which Mine exalted Pen hath revealed in My Most Holy Book that thou mayest hold fast unto it with such resolve and power as is born of Me; and I verily am the Ordainer, the All-Wise.

Great is indeed your blessedness inasmuch as His unfailing grace hath been vouchsafed unto you and ye have been aided to recognize this Cause—a Cause through whose potency the heavens have been folded together and every lofty and towering mountain hath been scattered in dust.

Moreover through Our boundless grace We make mention of your mother who hath been privileged to recognize God. We send her Our greetings from this glorious station. We remember every one of you, men and women, and from this Spot—the Scene of incomparable glory—regard you all as one soul and send you the joyous tidings of divine blessings which have preceded all created things, and of My remembrance that pervadeth everyone, whether young or old. The glory of God rest upon you, O people of Bahá. Rejoice with exceeding gladness through My remembrance, for He is indeed with you at all times.

Give ear unto that which the Spirit imparteth unto thee from the verses of God, the Help in Peril, the Self-Subsisting, that His Call may attract thee to the Summit of transcendent glory and draw thee nigh unto the Station where thou shalt behold thine entire being set ablaze with the fire of the love of God in such wise that neither the ascendancy of the rulers nor the whisperings of their vassals can quench it, and thou wilt arise amidst the peoples of the world to celebrate the praise of thy Lord, the Possessor of Names. This is that which well beseemeth thee in this Day.

We will recount for thee the thing that hath happened in the past that thou mayest perceive the sweetness of this utterance and become aware of such events as have transpired in former times. Verily thy Lord is the Admonisher, the Gracious, the Best-Beloved.

Call thou to mind the days when He Who conversed with God tended, in the wilderness, the sheep of Jethro, His father-in-law. He hearkened unto the Voice of the Lord of mankind coming from the Burning Bush which had been raised above the Holy Land, exclaiming, 'O Moses! Verily I am God, thy Lord and the Lord of thy forefathers, Abraham, Isaac and Jacob.' He was so carried away by the captivating accent of the Voice that He detached Himself from the world and set out in the direction of Pharaoh and his people, invested with the power of thy Lord Who exerciseth sovereignty over all that hath been and shall be. The people of the world are now hearing that which Moses did hear, but they understand not.

Say, I swear by the righteousness of God! Ere long the pomp of the ministers of state and the ascendancy of the rulers shall pass away, the palaces of the potentates shall be laid waste and the imposing buildings of the emperors reduced to dust, but what shall endure is that which We have ordained for you in the Kingdom. It behoveth you, O people, to make the utmost endeavour that your names may be mentioned before the Throne and ye may bring forth that which will immortalize your memories throughout the eternity of God, the Lord of all being.

Remember thou on My behalf the loved ones in that land, convey My greetings to them and gladden their hearts with the tidings of that which hath been revealed for them from this glorious station.

Say, take heed lest the overpowering might of the oppressors alarm you. The day is approaching when every emblem of vainglory will have been reduced to nothingness; then shall ye behold the invincible sovereignty of your Lord ruling over all things visible and invisible.

Beware lest the veils deter you from the outpourings of His bounty in this Day. Cast away the things that keep you back from God and persevere on this far-stretching Way. We desire naught for you but that which profiteth you as hath been recorded in His Preserved Tablet. We often remember Our loved ones; however, We have found them wanting in that which becometh them at the Court of the favour of their Lord, the Gracious, the Forgiving, save those whom God desireth to exempt. Verily, potent is He to do what He willeth. He giveth and withholdeth. He is indeed the Eternal Truth, the Knower of things unseen.

Seize ye, O loved ones of the All-Merciful, the chalice of eternal life proffered by the hand of the bountiful favours of your Lord, the Possessor of the entire creation, then drink ye deep therefrom. I swear by God, it will so enrapture you that ye shall arise to magnify His Name and proclaim His utterances amidst the peoples of the earth and shall conquer the cities of the hearts of men in the name of your Lord, the Almighty, the All-Praised.

Moreover, We announce unto everyone the joyful tidings concerning that which We have revealed in Our Most Holy Book—a Book from above whose horizon the day-star of My commandments shineth upon every observer and every observed one. Hold ye fast unto it and fulfil that which is revealed therein. Indeed better is this for you than whatsoever hath been created in the world, did ye but know it. Beware lest the transitory things of human life withhold you from turning unto God, the True One. Ponder ye in your hearts the world and its conflicts and changes, so that ye may discern its merit and the station of those who have set their hearts upon it and have turned away from that which hath been sent down in Our Preserved Tablet.

Thus have We revealed these holy verses and sent them unto thee that thou mayest arise to glorify the Name of God, the Help in Peril, the Self-Subsisting. The glory of God be upon thee and upon such as have partaken of this choice, sealed Wine.

THIS Wronged One hath perused thy letter in the Most Great Prison and is apprised of thine enquiry concerning the commandments of God on the subjects of resurrection and the means of livelihood. Thou hast done well to ask these questions, for the benefit thereof will be gained by thyself as well as other servants of God, both outwardly and inwardly. Verily thy Lord knoweth all things and readily answereth the call.

The supreme cause for creating the world and all that is therein is for man to know God. In this Day whosoever is guided by the fragrance of the raiment of His mercy to gain admittance into the pristine Abode, which is the station of recognizing the Source of divine commandments and the Dayspring of His Revelation, hath everlastingly attained unto all good. Having reached this lofty station a twofold obligation resteth upon every soul. One is to be steadfast in the Cause with such steadfastness that were all the peoples of the world to attempt to prevent him from turning to the Source of Revelation, they would be powerless to do so. The other is observance of the divine ordinances which have streamed forth from the wellspring of His heavenly-propelled Pen. For man's knowledge of God cannot develop fully and adequately save by observing whatsoever hath been ordained by Him and is set forth in His heavenly Book.

A year ago the Most Holy Book was sent down from the heaven of the bounty of the Lord of Names. God willing, thou mayest be graciously enabled to fulfil that which hath been revealed therein.

Concerning the means of livelihood, thou shouldst, while placing thy whole trust in God, engage in some occupation. He will assuredly send down upon thee from the heaven of His favour that which is destined for thee. He is in truth the God of might and power.

Yield thou thanks unto God that thy letter hath reached the presence of this Prisoner and from the Seat of divine authority the answer hath been revealed and is being sent to thee. This is an incalculable blessing vouchsafed by God. Although it is not evident at present, it soon shall be. It behoveth thee to say:

Magnified be Thy Name, O Lord my God! I am the one

who hath turned his face towards Thee and hath placed his whole reliance in Thee. I implore Thee by Thy Name whereby the ocean of Thine utterance hath surged and the breezes of Thy knowledge have stirred, to grant that I may be graciously aided to serve Thy Cause and be inspired to remember Thee and praise Thee. Send down then upon me from the heaven of Thy generosity that which will preserve me from anyone but Thee and will profit me in all Thy worlds.

Verily, Thou art the Powerful, the Inaccessible, the Supreme, the Knowing, the Wise.

NOTES

PASSAGES TRANSLATED BY SHOGHI EFFENDI

Wherever possible, translations made by Shoghi Effendi have been used in preparing this book. In many instances his renderings of individual phrases have been incorporated, but these are too numerous to list. Below are listed two categories of translation that have been used. One is a direct translation of the actual Tablet concerned, or of excerpts therefrom. The second category is slightly less direct: in a number of His later Writings Bahá'u'lláh used to quote passages from His own Tablets, but when doing so He often modified the passage from which He was quoting. Thus, when Shoghi Effendi's translations of such quoted passages—as, for example, in the *Epistle to the Son of the Wolf*—have been used, they have had to be adjusted to agree with the passage as it appeared in the Tablet from which Bahá'u'lláh was quoting, as it is these original Tablets that are here translated. Such adjustments are slight and have not been specially noted, but will be apparent to anyone who compares the passages as they appear in this book with the volumes from which Shoghi Effendi's translations are taken.

Abbreviations

ADJ	*The Advent of Divine Justice*
ESW	*Epistle to the Son of the Wolf*
GPB	*God Passes By*
GWB	*Gleanings from the Writings of Bahá'u'lláh*
HWA	*The Hidden Words* (In Arabic)
PDC	*The Promised Day Is Come*
SW	*Star of the West* (An early periodical in which a number of Shoghi Effendi's first translations were published)
WOB	*The World Order of Bahá'u'lláh* (A compilation of letters by Shoghi Effendi written between 1929 and 1936)

INDEX

INDEX